GROUNDCOVER
REVOLUTION

GROUNDCOVER
REVOLUTION

How to use sustainable, low-maintenance,
low-water groundcovers to replace your turf

KATHY JENTZ

author of *The Urban Garden*

COOL
SPRINGS
PRESS

Brimming with creative inspiration, how-to projects, and useful information to enrich your everyday life, quarto.com is a favorite destination for those pursuing their interests and passions.

First Published in 2023 by Cool Springs Press, an imprint of The Quarto Group, 100 Cummings Center, Suite 265-D, Beverly, MA 01915, USA.
T (978) 282-9590 F (978) 283-2742 Quarto.com

Cool Springs Press titles are also available at discount for retail, wholesale, promotional, and bulk purchase. For details, contact the Special Sales Manager by email at specialsales@quarto.com or by mail at The Quarto Group, Attn: Special Sales Manager, 100 Cummings Center, Suite 265-D, Beverly, MA 01915, USA.

27 26 25 24 23   1 2 3 4 5

ISBN: 978-0-7603-7815-1

Digital edition published in 2023
eISBN: 978-0-7603-7816-8

Library of Congress Cataloging-in-Publication Data available

Design: Allison Meierding
Cover Image: [front] Shutterstock; [back] Kathy Jentz, except Shutterstock (top right)
Page Layout: Allison Meierding
Illustration: Holly Neel

Printed in China
Printed in USA

CONTENTS

1 WHY REPLACE TURFGRASS LAWNS

"Groundcovers are nature's carpet that clothe the soil in a variety of green array and make this flowering world all the brighter and more beautiful."

–DANIEL J. FOLEY

Despite their appearance, our lawns are not the "green" expanses we think they are. Sure, they are better than concrete, but barely. In many instances, turfgrass lawns are so compacted and dense that storm water is hardly absorbed—causing most of it to run off into nearby streets and pollute local waterways with the herbicides, pesticides, and fertilizers that are applied to the turfgrass.

Consider all the maintenance costs of a turfgrass lawn. Frequent mowing, fertilizing, weeding, watering, reseeding, edging, and aerating not only eat up your personal resources of time and money, but they can be harsh on the environment. Even using all electric equipment and organic methods requires a far greater use of resources to maintain a "healthy" green lawn in comparison to nonturf groundcover alternatives.

Without your constant care (or that of a hired service), your yard filled with turfgrass can quickly become a drab brown mess. In a typical temperate climate yard, turfgrass turns to straw during the height of summer and then goes dormant again in the winter. In harsher climates, turfgrass is sometimes spray-painted and dyed green or even replaced with a plastic imitation carpet. All of this effort is done with the goal of having that "perfect" green lawn.

If you are reading this book, it is likely that turfgrass lawns are something you've struggled with. Perhaps you are weary of battling encroaching weeds and attacking insects. You likely are leery of using chemical lawn additives and are concerned about their impact on the planet. Maybe you just want those long lawn-maintenance hours back to devote to more compelling pursuits.

◀ The small entrance path to a home is framed by dwarf mondo grass and black mondo grass in an elegant and low-maintenance design.

Many homeowners only ever step foot on their lawn to mow it. They mainly experience their yards by looking out over them from inside their house. They are likely only maintaining a turfgrass lawn because that is what was always there, and they haven't considered easier options.

In this book, I will outline some easier, more attractive and Earth-friendly alternatives to the traditional turfgrass lawn. Before we delve deeper, I want to make it clear that I am not completely anti-lawn. There are times when turfgrass makes sense in a landscape such as for a play area for children or pets.

However, there is a pervasive overuse of turfgrass in home landscapes that is both illogical and unhealthy. History has proven that widespread use of a monoculture is almost always a tragedy waiting to happen. Once a disease or pest targets that plant, it can spread like wildfire. From the loss of American elms to the Irish Potato Famine, we have learned that diversity in landscapes and plant choices is the key to their health and survival.

Perhaps you like the look of a lawn? A landscape made of groundcover plants can create a similar green expanse but in a much more efficient and eco-wise way. Turfgrass may struggle to grow under a large shade tree, under heavy foot traffic, or in an excessively wet area. There are specific groundcovers that thrive in each of these conditions, and they can help fill those problem locations in your landscape.

Steep slopes and hills are another location where turfgrass is not the optimal choice. In fact, it is dangerous to mow these sites as a loss of traction and stability can risk injuring the operator. One could even safely say that groundcovers could save your life!

▶ A low border of Bugleweed (*Ajuga reptans*) groundcover separates a turfgrass lawn from a perennial bed.

The Definition of a Groundcover

What is a groundcover? A narrow definition of a groundcover would be a plant that spreads across the ground and only grows a few inches high. Under these restrictions, only those creeping, mat-forming plants would qualify. The broader definition of a groundcover is any plant that sufficiently covers the soil in a fairly dense manner. Groundcovers are characteristically perennials, though there are a number of low-growing shrubs that qualify. I'd expand that definition to also include self-sowing annuals, sprawling vines, and ornamental grasses.

The groundcovers discussed in this book are those selections that are viable substitutes for turfgrass lawns. They are low-maintenance, moderately fast spreaders, and don't require a lot of chemical applications to flourish.

THERE IS NO SUCH THING AS NO-MAINTENANCE

One extreme option some homeowners have taken when frustrated with their turfgrass is replacing it with artificial turf or even pouring concrete over their yards. While lower maintenance than a lawn, these substitutes are environmentally harmful. The chemicals used to create and apply them break down over time and enter the soil, and the impervious surfaces exacerbate the stormwater run-off problems in a landscape even further. Some local governments are even levying taxes on impervious hardscape surfaces to mitigate the community's shared costs in dealing with their effects.

Placing nonbreathable hardscaping over tree roots and living soil in effect kills both. Further, they are not "no maintenance." As a matter of fact, they may not even be low-maintenance. Hard surfaces accumulate litter and debris. They must be swept or blown clean regularly. Spilled materials show up embarrassingly on concrete like lipstick stains on a collar. A concrete driveway needs the occasional resealing/repair and snow needs to be shoveled off when it piles up.

The average lifespan of artificial grass is only 10 years, and the cost to install or replace it is not small. It requires regular raking to spruce up any matted down sections. It holds onto and traps in heat, pollution particles, and smells from pet waste. The underlayment material is often even more problematic than the plastic grass itself as it can contain byproducts and discards of industry.

▲ Creeping thyme makes an ideal groundcover for next sections to paved areas that receive lots of foot and vehicular traffic.

MY PERSONAL GROUNDCOVER JOURNEY

My garden journey began in a ground floor condominium apartment that had a deeply shaded walk-out patio. I filled every nook and cranny of that shady patio with containers overflowing with flowering plants. I started by hanging them from the upper apartment's balcony and the nearby porch railings, then I began creeping out into the common grounds of the condominium complex. Placing one pot at a time along the walkway leading to my unit and digging in extra plants around nearby shrubs and trees. At that point, the condo board said, "Enough." They urged me to stay within my own unit's bounds, but my gardening passion couldn't be held back. After a few more slaps on the hand for exceeding my own property, I decided it was time to find more space in which to garden.

So, I purchased a small brick home on a busy urban corner. One side was shaded by huge old oak trees and the other was in full sun.

▲ The all-turfgrass portion of my corner landscape was converted in just a few years to lush groundcover plantings that include groundcover roses, daylilies, black-eyed Susans, iris, and more.

▲ When life gives you a solid English ivy groundcover, make lemonade out of your lemons—making light of it and placing plastic yard flamingos in the bed until you get a chance to transition the area to a noninvasive groundcover.

The shaded portion had a solid groundcover of English ivy on a mainly flat area, while the full sun part on a sloping corner location was covered with a thick turfgrass lawn. The first time I tried to mow the sunny slope with a reel push mower, I nearly collapsed from heat stroke. I gave up and hired a mow-and-blow crew to keep the lawn in check that first year, while I decorated the home's interior. Every time I looked out the window, I cursed that lawn. I wanted swaths of cheery flowers buzzing with pollinators, not a lifeless expanse of blah that not only gave me no satisfaction or joy, but actually cost me money and time to maintain.

The second year, I decided to tackle the lawn and replace it. I dug up sections and planted shrubs, perennials, and small trees. Then I discovered the miracle of groundcovers. I attended a garden club plant swap and a fellow member offered up a fast-spreading plant that she warned would soon blanket the ground. Sold! From then on, every plant sale, swap, and nursery that I attended I looked for the keywords of "aggressive," "thug," and "rampant" on the plant's description. By the third year, all the turfgrass lawn was gone and I had several swaths of competing perennial groundcovers surrounding the flowering shrubs and small trees.

I then turned my attention to the full shade portion of my landscape. I took out a huge chunk of it and situated a small gazebo in the middle of the circle of oak trees. Then I started beating back the edges of the English ivy. This task was not an easy one and is still going on today. After more than a decade of frequent battles with the ivy, I am winning, but much more slowly than the turfgrass war.

I planted a series of shade-loving groundcovers in place of the ivy where I pulled it. Constant vigilance is required to not to have the ivy take over again. In other spots, I have dug out a circle in the middle of a small ivy patch and inserted a shade groundcover to see who will dominate. The shade-loving groundcovers that can hold their own against the ivy and even overrun it include Solomon's seal, Christmas fern, lily-of-the-valley, cranesbill geranium, and epimedium. Others, like hellebores, hostas, and heucheras, need assistance to keep ivy from choking them out again.

These lessons and more are the basis of this book, and I continue to experiment with plant combinations to see which groundcovers best survive adverse conditions, behave well around neighboring plantings, or do battle with the ivy. I welcome your experiences and feedback as your own journey to growing more groundcovers expands. If you have a trick or plant pick you want to share, email me anytime at kathyjentz@gmail.com.

2 BENEFITS OF GROUNDCOVERS

When you start to explore the world of turfgrass alternatives, your initial focus might be only on getting the open ground covered quickly and establishing a viable replacement. Then, all the wonderful possibilities will start to present themselves. Not only can you be free of lawn maintenance headaches, but you can also support your local ecosystem. You are saving money and your landscape is suddenly more interesting and beautiful. And you are conserving water and stopping soil erosion and frequent flooding after rainstorms. In this chapter, we'll explore some of the bonus benefits of installing groundcover plants.

WEED SUPPRESSION

One of the constant aggravations of turfgrass lawns is dealing with so-called "weeds" that insinuate themselves into the ideal environment you are providing for them. When you cut turfgrass blades at a low height, you allow sunlight to reach the soil and that encourages weed seeds to germinate. When you water and fertilize the grass, you are also doing the same for the weeds. It is futile to fight the wind-born seeds, instead you need to create an environment that is hostile to their establishment. Weeds are opportunistic. Give them an inch and they gladly will take it and run a mile.

Established groundcovers help reduce weeds by creating a solid, healthy mat of roots. They grow thickly to shade the soil and prevent weed seed germination. Some groundcovers are better at weed suppression than others. If this is a main goal of yours, select groundcovers with dense, low foliage that forms a thick mat on the surface of the soil. Examples of these include *Ajuga, Brunnera*, and most any plant with "creeping" in the common name (more specifics about these varieties can be found in chapter 5).

◄ Low groundcovers can fill in around ornamental garden features or where turfgrass doesn't grow well.

FILL IN DEEP SHADE
OR FULL SUN

Turfgrass struggles in deep shade and can also do poorly in full sun, especially in warmer climates. Many groundcover plants are suitable for either situation, though very few do well in both of these extremes. Therefore, I recommend thinking of each groundcover choice as a tailored fit rather than a one-size-fits-all approach. It may take a wardrobe of several kinds of groundcovers mixed together to create a patchwork that covers all the portions of your landscape.

This need not look a crazy quilt, unless you happen to like that colorful appearance! (See more about that option in the Installing and Maintaining Groundcovers chapter.) One area can transition gradually into the other with one groundcover increasingly mixing in with another. For instance, a deep shade area of moss could gently give way to a mass of wild violets or wild ginger.

In full sun, you might plant several flowering perennial groundcovers in masses of three feet (91 cm) diameters side by side. This effectively is a meadow planting, though a very controlled one. A few good choices for this application would include black-eyed Susans, lamb's ear, and clumps of tall ornamental grasses such as *Panicum virgatum*, *Andropogon gerardii*, *Schizachyrium scoparium*, and *Sorghastrum nutans*.

You could also deliberately separate groundcovers in one growing situation from another one with landscape features such as a pathway or retaining wall. This method can also help to keep one kind of groundcover from running roughshod over another. (More on this technique in the Installing and Maintaining Groundcovers chapter.)

▲ Turfgrass fails in deep shade, while moss is the perfect plant for this situation. It is soft underfoot, lovely to the eye, and virtually no-maintenance.

◄ One of the many benefits of a healthy and full groundcover planting is that it prevents any weed seeds for germinating on exposed soils.

▲ Flowering groundcovers support bees, butterflies, and other beneficial insects.

WILDLIFE SUPPORT

Many groundcover plants produce flowers. We love the beauty of flowers, but they also provide nectar and pollen for beneficial insects. The flowers then turn into seedheads and feed birds. There's no need to put up and fill commercial birdfeeders when your whole landscape is one!

Certain groundcovers provide more pollinator support than others. Some are host plants for the larval stage of specific insects or they are so floriferous that they are essentially super-feeders. I have highlighted these wildlife support groundcovers in the plant listings and the reference chart later in this book.

Additional wildlife benefits of groundcovers include providing shelter from bad weather and predators, as well as providing nesting materials for birds and other creatures.

ABSORB STORMWATER AND BUILD SOILS

I have already touched on the superior ability of groundcover plants to absorb stormwater over that done by turfgrass lawns. Groundcovers can also act as a filter for pollutants and take in excess nutrients as well. After they intercept the water, they transpire the moisture back out over several days. Increased groundcover foliage density equals increased absorption and transpiration. Also, the ground shading by these plants also prevents quick water evaporation on hot days.

A number of groundcover plantings establish deeper roots than turfgrass—these can better combat soil erosion especially on sloped landscapes. The groundcovers collect organic debris and break it down adding to the healthy and diverse soil biology as well.

Groundcover plants blanket the soil and hold fallen leaves, seeds, and twigs. On a turfgrass lawn these would be raked and bagged up and sent to a landfill. Held in a groundcover, they break down and add organic materials back to the soil. It is the natural cycle of how plants feed each other and themselves. With this process restored, there is no need for applications of artificial fertilizers.

Planting groundcovers around your home's foundation also has the benefit of taking in excess water from gutters and eaves. The groundcovers stop the heavy rains from splashing mud back onto your home and nearby pathways.

▲ Ferns make the ideal groundcover for swales and other spots in the landscape that stay damp all the time.

LIVING OR GREEN "MULCH"

Groundcovers act as a living or green mulch on the soil. Taller plants such as shrubs and trees benefit from having green mulches in their root zones. They help hold in moisture and insulate from temperature extremes. Living mulches suppress weeds and hold down soils, preventing erosion.

Certain garden plants, such as clematis and lilies, like their root zones to be shaded and groundcovers serve this function well. Other perennials, such as peonies, may be slow to fill in and groundcovers will hold their garden spots for them until they do fill in.

Further, avoiding running machines over the root zones of larger plants prevents soil compaction and mechanical injury such as cuts on their trunks that can introduce disease and pest issues.

Planting green mulches saves gardeners from having to reapply brown mulches each growing season. A short aside here to also note that using mulch as a decorative element is frowned upon in landscape design circles. The practice of placing a plant in a ring of mulch and then another one near it and so on, isolating each plant in its own mulch hell is not only unnatural, but wasteful and frankly bizarre. The plants do not benefit from growing in isolation and in fact naturally grow in groupings and colonies. (Do not get me started on the harmful practices of piling mulch up a tree trunk or applying dyed or rubber mulches around living plants!) These misguided applications of mulch are not for the plant's health nor are they considered attractive, instead they evolved because they are the easiest way for work crews to quickly apply mounds of mulch and maintain a landscape on their schedule and at their convenience, not for the optimal benefit of the plantings they are supposedly taking caring of.

▲ The different foliage colors and textures in this mixture of various shade-loving groundcovers is quite attractive.

SOLVING LANDSCAPE CHALLENGES

Groundcovers are the perfect solution for parts of your landscape that are tough to grow in or maintain. Rocky, steep, or inaccessible portions of your yard are best turned over to a colony of plants that can cover these spots and do so beautifully.

Difficult areas might include narrow strips and between large items such as cable boxes—tight spaces make access for easy weeding and maintenance an issue—where mowers may not fit. A small groundcover can be tucked in almost anywhere; low-growing sedums are especially useful for this.

The area around thorny plants is another space where weeding and maintenance can be a headache. If you love roses, do yourself a favor and plant a green carpet of creeping rosemary under them.

Groundcovers also serve to soften the edges of steps and hardscaping. They can also denote changes in elevation in the landscape with different textures or colors calling attention to changes in grade thereby making the yard safer to enjoy.

Invasive plants can be kept in check by using the right groundcovers. Epimedium is one that I have found holds its ground and even swallows up English ivy and Japanese honeysuckle runners.

(Also see the section in the next chapter on Natives Versus Nonnatives.)

▼ Groundcovers don't always have to be on the ground. They can be used on green roofs and walls as well as in elevated planters to be low-maintenance and attractive fillers.

UNIQUE APPLICATIONS

Groundcovers fill in niche spots that no other plants are capable of occupying. From miniature gardens to the little gaps between pavers and at the base of sheds or other outbuildings, low-growing groundcovers can squeeze into almost any garden spot.

If a crack in your driveway can support a weed, pull it and pop in a piece of a groundcover plant. Tuck them into gaps in stone walls and retaining walls.

Save some leftover segments of creeping groundcovers for fun projects like a teacup garden or a terrarium.

AMENDING TOUGH SOILS

Clay soil can be a challenge as it is nutrient-rich, though not well-draining. Groundcover plants that can tolerate sitting in moist spots are good to plant in heavy clay soils. Also recommended are groundcover plants with clay-busting deep roots such as dwarf comfrey.

Compacted soil is common where a turfgrass lawn has been growing for decades. Similar to clay-busting plants, look for groundcovers that have deep tap roots that can break up dense soils and amend then.

▲ Low-growing groundcovers are the perfect backdrop for a fairy garden. They are also useful in garden railways and other miniature-scale gardens.

▲ Moisture-loving groundcovers thrive in clay soils and other wet garden conditions.

TREE ROOT COMPANIONS

Tree roots are challenging to work around and mow over. You don't want to harm the tree by layering thick mulch on top of its roots, but the root zone area can become weedy if left un-planted. They need to breathe and have access to rainwater. A taller groundcover like ferns is a good choice to plant in this spot. The ferns can swallow dropped leaves and hold moisture in that location.

Tree roots are sometimes a tripping hazard. Covering them with plantings discourages people from walking in that location and protects the roots from heavy foot traffic.

▲ Shallow-rooted groundcovers are a practical solution for planting in tree boxes and around tree root zones.

Quick Tip

Before removing turfgrass or other plantings from an area where you want to install groundcovers, check the weather and clear your schedule. Have a plan ready to plant the groundcovers as soon as possible, so that you don't cause a muddy, run-off erosion mess when it next rains.

3

HOW TO SELECT THE RIGHT GROUNDCOVER FOR YOUR SITUATION

The chart, **Groundcovers and Their Properties** at the end of this chapter on pages 42–47 will assist you in your selection process of which groundcover will do best in each growing condition in your landscape. In this chapter, the chart's terms and classifications are defined and detailed. A quick perusal of these ratings and their reasoning will help you to better understand your own growing conditions and the qualities you seek in a groundcover.

Some of these categories may not have occurred to you to be a criteria in your groundcover search. Maybe you never considered choosing a turfgrass replacement on its salt-tolerance or wildlife benefit, but I hope that these give you the options you seek and assist in your decision-making process.

◀ A mix of easy-care groundcovers surrounds this small water feature in a private garden.

So Many Plants, So Few Pages

I could have made this book two or three times the size you are reading now. The plant listing might easily have been a top 100 or more of great groundcover plants, but limits are a good thing—in both gardening and publishing. With a strict word count and page length, my wise project editor and I settled on a top 40 selection to share in this volume.

The plants that made the cut here are those that I have personally grown and had success with. My own climate is temperate (USDA Zone 7) in the Mid-Atlantic United States. We get all four seasons here with weather extremes from cold winter freezes to hot, humid summers—from summer-long droughts to rainy, wet springs. The plants included here are tough work-horses that survive my "set it and forget it" method. If they can not only survive my virtual neglect, but thrive, they get a thumbs up from me.

As with all gardening, your local climate will dictate your plant choices and your "mileage may vary" as they say with these same plants. I tried to include a wide variety to address all possible growing conditions from blazing hot and dry to cool and wet. There may be no one groundcover that will address all of your needs, but several will hopefully come close. I suggest you trial a few candidates first in select spots, then expand on those that show the most promise and success.

The most frequent question I am asked is for what I call the "unicorn"—the perfect groundcover. They want a groundcover that is: native to the person's region, deer/pest/disease-proof, evergreen, drought-tolerant and can handle wet feet, and, of course, no-mainte-nance. The closest contenders I have found for unicorn status in my region are creeping junipers, cranesbill geraniums, and Christmas ferns. My overall ground-cover champion choice for best all-around performer is epimedium, although it is not native to my area.

One or more plants in the listings should fit your particular needs. Still there are many plants that I wish I could have included here. (Perhaps these are one of your favorites?) Species that were almost included include: creeping mazus (*Mazus reptans*), pinks (*Dianthus* spp.), strawberry begonia (*Saxifraga stolonifera*), rose campion (*Silene coronaria*), silver carpet (*Dymondia margaretae*), and blue-eyed grass (*Sisyrinchium angustifolium*). You may wish to do your own reading and research on these almost-included groundcovers to see if they might work for you. There are hundreds of other groundcover choices not named here, I encourage you to explore your local gardening experts and resources to see what choices they have success with and recommend.

▲ Creeping mazus (Mazus reptans) is a low-growing perennial plant that makes an ideal groundcover in fertile soils that are consistently moist.

▶ Edible plants such as basil and chard are mixed in with a low-growing groundcover.

Sun Versus Shade

A plant's tag or catalog description indicates the range of sun exposure a plant can tolerate. This is often a broad range and does not indicate the plant's optimal growing conditions. In the plant profile section in chapter 5, you will find a description of the ideal sun exposure preferred by that plant category.

Full sun means 6-8 hours of direct sunlight per day. Part-sun and part-shade are generally used to mean 4-6 hours of sunlight. Full shade means less than 4 hours of sunlight. Note that full shade does not equate to no sunlight at all. No groundcover plant can survive in absolute darkness.

In the Groundcovers and Their Properties chart classifications, a groundcover that prefers full sun conditions indicates "yes." If it can survive in full sun, but that is not its ideal conditions, it states "somewhat." If it cannot tolerate full sun, the chart specifies, "no." The same criteria are used for the part-sun/part-shade and full shade ratings.

If you are unsure of the amount of hours of sunlight that a location in your landscape received, you can use a light meter or light exposure paper to measure it. Spend a day observing the area's conditions every couple of hours.

Natives Versus Nonnative

Many homeowners are seeking to eliminate turfgrass lawns and replace them with native plantings. Native plants can support local wildlife including providing seeds for songbirds and nectar for butterflies. Plants that are native to a growing region *may* also require less maintenance and inputs (water, fertilizer, etc.). It is a fallacy though, that they do not need watering or any other supplemental support. Like all plants, native plants should be matched to your specific growing conditions.

For the purposes of this book, the "native" range of a plant is listed by the continent it originates from. Many plants referenced in our listings have native species in multiple places around the world. The section on Noteworthy Cultivars and Varieties in each listing goes into more detail about individual plant choices.

Note however that these plants may not be native to your own eco-region, or it may be that only one specific variety is native to your area. If using native plants is of particular concern for you, you will want to research your plant choices and sources carefully. Seek out specialty native plant sellers and ask them where the native plants originated from and even enquire about the best native solutions to your groundcover challenges. In many cases, the exact origin of a plant variety or cultivar may not be known. You will need to use the next best option available.

▶ Some groundcovers may be listed as "full sun or part sun" on their plant labels, but they will need protection from the harshest afternoon sunlight in hot growing regions. For example, this epimedium does best in morning sun and afternoon shade.

Fast Spreading

Groundcover plants are by definition those that grow relatively quickly and spread out over the soil. In some cases, they can out-compete other plants and this makes them ideal for blocking out weeds and creating the pleasing appearance of a solid, filled-out area of healthy plant growth.

These same traits that make them great groundcovers can also be troublesome when combined in mixed border plantings with other, less-vigorous specimens. As a result, you may hear them referred to as "garden thugs," rampant, invasive, or aggressive. In garden catalog marketing, the more polite term is fast spreading. You may also see these plants called "stoloniferous" or said to "spread readily through rhizomes." That is, they propagate themselves by underground root runners.

The terms "aggressive" and "invasive" are often used interchangeably when referring to certain plants. They are not synonyms and should not be used carelessly. An aggressive plant is any fast-growing plant. (It can also refer to one that readily self-sows itself about via prolific seed dispersal.) An invasive plant may be aggressive as well, but this term should only be applied to those plants that have been identified by horticultural authorities as dangerous, exotic (nonnative) plants that may negatively impact a local ecosystem.

▲ Placing equally aggressively spreading groundcovers next to each other keeps one from running rampant over the rest.

One plant may be invasive in a certain growing area and may be perfectly well-behaved in another region. This book uses the list of invasive plants created by the USDA National Invasive Species Information Center (NISIC) as the authority to determine a plant's invasive status in the North American continent. Any plant determined as invasive in the listing at www.invasivespeciesinfo.gov was automatically eliminated for consideration as a groundcover option in the book listings. In particular, you will not find English ivy (*Hedera helix*) suggested in these pages.

◄ A bed of perennial plants transitions from low groundcovers in the front to taller, flowering selections toward the back.

▲ Why fight it? Let moss establish itself into a lawn where the growing conditions are shady and damp.

▲ For a visually pleasing effect, mix two groundcovers with opposite foliage shapes.

Drought-Tolerant or Tolerates Soggy Soils

In the Groundcovers and Their Properties comparison chart, I rated plants as yes/somewhat/no for being drought-tolerant and tolerating soggy soils. Alas, there are very few plants in cultivation that tolerate both conditions well.

For assessing your needs, know that both terms are relative and what is considered dry versus moist soil is very different in various climates. My desperately dry June may be your annual average rainfall.

A drought-tolerance rating of "yes" is generally seasonal and doesn't indicate a totally dry or desert-like landscape. Dry shade under deciduous trees is one common example, where plants may withstand a hot, rain-less summer and bounce back with sufficiently wet winters.

On the other hand, soggy soils can be a boggy site or a low-lying part of your landscape that collects water after a storm and is slow draining. Plants that prefer or don't mind wet feet for long periods of time are rated as "yes" in the chart.

Flowering or Foliage Interest

Plants rated "yes" for foliage interest or flowering are known for this feature. Foliage interest can denote an attractive leaf shape, fall color, or interesting texture. "Somewhat" for foliage interest may indicate a small or narrow leaf that is not of much visual interest.

Flowering is a bit more straightforward. A rating of "somewhat" may mean that the flowers are sporadic or fleeting. A "no" rating means that the flowers are insignificant or barely noticeable.

▲ Some groundcovers, such as Hostas, dieback and disappear in the winter. This effect is known affectionately amongst gardeners as the "mouse graveyard."

Evergreen or Deciduous

Evergreen does not mean the plant stays green forever. A rating of "yes" for evergreen may not apply to the coldest of climates or if you experience an unusually frigid winter one year. Even if the leaves or needles stay on year-round, there will still be an annual renewal process. With most plants that means in late winter or early spring, the old foliage will be worn and tattered. Cut it back to allow the newly emerging foliage to grow up.

Salt Tolerant

The salt-tolerant rating is of importance to those who live near the ocean, but also impacts those that live in cold winter climates where streets are salted for road traction. The salt trucks often overspray and apply salt to the surrounding plantings on sidewalk edges and medians, where many homeowners plant low-maintenance groundcovers.

▲ Salt spread on icy sidewalks and roadways impacts adjacent plantings.

▲ Layer groundcovers from low to high along walkways and at the front of planting beds.

▲ Rabbits love white clover and will choose it over most any other plant in your garden.

Tall

A "yes" rating in the tall column of the chart denotes a plant whose flowers or foliage is above knee height, while a "somewhat" rating can mean a plant has basal foliage that hugs to ground most of the year, but sends up a tall flower spike for a month or so. "Somewhat" can also mean it depends on the cultivar or variety. Some plants, such as black-eyed Susans, have very tall and also dwarf selections.

Deer Resistant and Wildlife Benefit

Deer-resistance ratings are based on feedback from a number of growers and breeders. However, every deer population develops its own regional tastes and foraging habits. They will also eat things that are poisonous and that they are "not supposed to" when they are hungry enough, as any starving creature world. There is no such thing as deer-proof. Every deer born must also learn that a bite of a hellebore leaf is bitter and after a few does use your plantings to teach that lesson, you may have little left. Deer also cause plant damage in other ways—by using it as bedding or by rubbing their antlers on it.

The wildlife benefit rating mainly means a plant supports beneficial pollinators such as honeybees, native bees, and butterflies. It can also mean it is a larval food source for beneficial insects. That can mean you will experience some defoliation of the groundcover, but not enough that it will harm the plant's health or be too unsightly. Another wildlife benefit could be as cover or a seed source for ground-nesting birds. If rated as "yes," the exact wildlife benefit is described in the plant listings in chapter 5.

▲ Drought-resistant plantings save water and are often fire resistant as well.

Fire-Wise

This category rating is a reflection of an increasing risk in our modern world of wildfire dangers. Plants rated here as "yes" or "somewhat" fire-wise should be considered for those in areas where wildfires are becoming more frequent. The fire-wise rating should also be examined for those outside those regions as a potential deciding factor between two otherwise equal groundcover options.

Leaf Swallowing

A growing movement to "leave the leaves" is urging homeowners to not rake up and dispose of leaves from their landscapes in the fall. Instead, homeowners are asked to leave them in place until early the following spring when the beneficial insects that over-winter in them have emerged.

The side-benefit to this is that the leaves will eventually break down and add nutrients back into the soil for the surrounding plants to use.

The drawback to this is that leaves left on turfgrass lawns will kill the lawn. Those with turfgrass lawns or groundcovers rated a "no" in this category can instead rake the leaves off and pile them in a side location to break down into compost to use as a mulch the next year.

Groundcovers rated as "yes" for leaf-swallowing are efficient at capturing large quantities of fallen leaves and holding them to break-down among their foliage. These plants are prime picks for planting under deciduous trees. Those rated "somewhat" can handle some light leaf fall, but would likely be overwhelmed by a mature tree's worth of leaves being dumped on them.

▲ Even low-growing groundcovers can handle a heavy leaf load—allowing them to break down and add nutrition back to the soil.

▲ Clay-tolerant groundcovers will not rot or "melt" in these dense often compacted soils.

▲ Check your local growing zones to determine the best cold-hardy groundcovers for your area.

Clay Tolerant

A plant rated in the chart as "yes" for clay tolerance is one that is generally not picky about soil type and can thrive in heavy, compacted ground. A "somewhat" rating means the plant can grow in lighter, noncompacted clay soils, but would do better in humus-rich soils. A "no" rating means the plant will fail within a few years if planted in clay soil, usually due to root rot.

Cold Hardiness

The hardiness rating shows the coldest temperature that a plant can take and still survive. In this book, I have selected groundcovers that are at least hardy to 15°F (-9°C) to give a broad range of choices for temperate and cold climate gardeners. Some of the cultivars listed may not be as cold-hardy as the straight species and I have noted where that is the case for a particular selection.

A Note on Common Names

I have included the most-popular common names along with the Latin names of each profiled groundcover listed in this book, although I bet I missed many! Common names develop out of folk traditions and are passed down generation to generation. They are very localized and one region may call it one thing, while the neighboring one has a totally different term for the same plant.

Common names are also like that old game of telephone, where one learns a plant's name from another and wrong or right passes it on down the line, often changing a syllable or confusing two similar words. (How did creeping Jenny also get named creeping Charlie?)

Sometimes it is a matter of simple misunderstanding. I have witnessed homeowners pointing at one plant and the listener looking at an entirely different one, forever matching a wrong name to the plant they see in their mind.

When sourcing plants, the Latin name should be used whenever possible. At times though plant tags and catalog descriptions can also be at best vague ("sedum groundcover") or downright incorrect, such as the mislabeled heucheras called "hostas" in a big-box store chain's sales circulars. Then there are the tags that get dislodged from a pot at a retail nursery and placed back in the wrong one.

Proper identification is necessary so you can be sure you are not introducing an invasive near cousin of the groundcover you intended to select to your landscape and creating a future maintenance headache. An experienced gardener can help you sort things out as can online plant ID groups that allow you to upload photos to get a confirmation of your guess.

▲ Groundcovers with several common names lead to confusion in identifying and purchasing plants. Best to use the Latin names to avoid mix-ups.

GROUNDCOVERS AND THEIR PROPERTIES

The chart on the following pages will help you select the best groundcovers for your landscape. For detailed profiles of each of these groundcovers, head to chapter 5 on page 73.

Groundcover/ Botanical Name	Cold Hardiness	Drought-Tolerant	Tolerates Soggy Soils	Disease Resistant	Salt Tolerant	Clay Tolerant	Evergreen	Full Shade	Part-Shade/ Part-Sun	Full Sun
Begonia, Hardy *Begonia grandis*	-10°F (-23°C)									no
Black-eyed Susan *Rudbeckia* spp.	-25°F (-32°C)		no					no		
Brunnera *Brunnera macrophylla*	-35°F (-37°C)		no							no
Bugleweed *Ajuga reptans*	-35°F (-37°C)									
Comfrey, Dwarf *Symphytum ibericum*	-20°F (-30°C)						no			
Epimedium *Epimedium* spp.	-25°F (-32°C)				no					no
Fern, Christmas *Polystichum acrostichoides*	-35°F (-37°C)				no					
Fescue, Blue 'Elijah Blue' *Festuca glauca* 'Elijah Blue'	-25°F (-32°C)		somewhat					no		
Geranium, Cranesbill *Geranium macrorrhizum*	-25°F (-32°C)		somewhat							
Ginger, Wild *Asarum canadense*	-35°F (-37°C)	no			no					no
Green and Gold *Chrysogonum virginianum*	-20°F (-30°C)				no					
Hellebore *Helleborus* spp.	-20°F (-30°C)				no					no
Heuchera *Heuchera* spp.	-25°F (-32°C)									

yes

somewhat

no

Groundcover	Deer Resistant	Leaf Swallowing	Fast Spreading	Tall	Foliage Interest	Flowering	Wildlife Benefit	Fire-wise	Native Range
Begonia, Hardy *Begonia grandis*	■							■	Asia
Black-eyed Susan *Rudbeckia spp.*		■			■				North America
Brunnera *Brunnera macrophylla*		■							Europe/Asia
Bugleweed *Ajuga reptans*				■					Europe
Comfrey, Dwarf *Symphytum ibericum*									Europe
Epimedium *Epimedium spp.*							■		Asia/Europe
Fern, Christmas *Polystichum acrostichoides*						■			North America
Fescue, Blue 'Elijah Blue' *Festuca glauca 'Elijah Blue'*									Europe/Cultivar
Geranium, Cranesbill *Geranium macrorrhizum*									North America
Ginger, Wild *Asarum canadense*				■					North America
Green and Gold *Chrysogonum virginianum*		■	■	■					North America
Hellebore *Helleborus spp.*							■	■	Asia/Europe
Heuchera *Heuchera spp.*			■						North America

Groundcover/ Botanical Name	Cold Hardiness	Drought-Tolerant	Tolerates Soggy Soils	Disease Resistant	Salt Tolerant	Clay Tolerant	Evergreen	Full Shade	Part-Shade/ Part-Sun	Full Sun
Hosta *Hosta* spp.	-35°F (-37°C)									
Iris, Dwarf Crested *Iris cristata*	-35°F (-37°C)									
Jasmine, Winter *Jasminum nudiflorum*	-15°F (-26°C)									
Jenny, Creeping *Lysimachia nummularia*	-25°F (-32°C)									
Juniper, Creeping *Juniperus horizontalis*	-35°F (-37°C)									
Lamb's Ear *Stachys byzantina*	-25°F (-32°C)									
Lamium *Lamium maculatum*	-25°F (-32°C)									
Lily-of-the-Valley *Convallaria majalis*	-50°F (-45°C)									
Liriope *Liriope muscari*	-25°F (-32°C)									
Mondo Grass, Dwarf *Ophiopogon japonicus* 'Nanus'	-5°F (-20°C)									
Mosses *Hypnum* spp.	-25°F (-32°C)									
Pachysandra *Pachysandra procumbens*	-25°F (-32°C)									
Phlox, Creeping *Phlox stolonifera*	-15°F (-26°C)									
Prickly Pear *Opuntia* spp.	-25°F (-32°C)									

yes

somewhat

no

Groundcover	Deer Resistant	Leaf Swallowing	Fast Spreading	Tall	Foliage Interest	Flowering	Wildlife Benefit	Fire-wise	Native Range
Hosta *Hosta* spp.	●								Asia
Iris, Dwarf Crested *Iris cristata*				●					North America
Jasmine, Winter *Jasminum nudiflorum*									Asia
Jenny, Creeping *Lysimachia nummularia*		●		●			●	●	Europe
Juniper, Creeping *Juniperus horizontalis*			●	●		●		●	North America
Lamb's Ear *Stachys byzantina*									Asia/Europe
Lamium *Lamium maculatum*				●					Europe/Asia/Africa
Lily-of-the-Valley *Convallaria majalis*							●		Asia/Europe
Liriope *Liriope muscari*									Asia
Mondo Grass, Dwarf *Ophiopogon japonicus* 'Nanus'						●	●		Asia
Mosses *Hypnum* spp.		●	●	●			●		Worldwide
Pachysandra *Pachysandra procumbens*		●		●					North America
Phlox, Creeping *Phlox stolonifera*		●							North America
Prickly Pear *Opuntia* spp.		●	●						North America/Central America/South America

Groundcover/ Botanical Name	Cold Hardiness	Drought-Tolerant	Tolerates Soggy Soils	Disease Resistant	Salt Tolerant	Clay Tolerant	Evergreen	Full Shade	Part-Shade/ Part-Sun	Full Sun
Pussytoes *Antennaria* spp.	-35°F (-37°C)	yes	no	somewhat	no	somewhat	somewhat	somewhat	somewhat	yes
Quaker Ladies *Houstonia caerulea*	-35°F (-37°C)	no	yes	somewhat	yes	somewhat	somewhat	yes	yes	yes
Ragwort, Golden *Packera aurea*	-35°F (-37°C)	somewhat	somewhat	somewhat	somewhat	somewhat	somewhat	yes	yes	yes
Raspberry, Creeping *Rubus hayata-koidzumii*	-5°F (-20°C)	somewhat	no	somewhat	no	somewhat	somewhat	yes	yes	yes
River Oats *Chasmanthium latifolium*	-25°F (-32°C)	somewhat	somewhat	somewhat	somewhat	somewhat	somewhat	yes	yes	yes
Rosemary, Creeping *Salvia rosmarinus* 'Prostratus'	15°F (-9°C)	yes	no	somewhat	somewhat	no	yes	no	somewhat	yes
Roses, Groundcover *Rosa* spp.	-20°F (-30°C)	somewhat	no	somewhat	somewhat	somewhat	somewhat	no	somewhat	yes
Sedge, Japanese *Carex morrowii*	-15°F (-26°C)	somewhat	somewhat	somewhat	somewhat	somewhat	yes	yes	yes	somewhat
Sedge, Pennsylvania *Carex pensylvanica*	-35°F (-37°C)	yes	no	somewhat	somewhat	somewhat	somewhat	yes	yes	somewhat
Solomon's Seal *Polygonatum* spp.	-35°F (-37°C)	somewhat	somewhat	somewhat	somewhat	somewhat	no	yes	yes	no
Stonecrop *Sedum ternatum*	-35°F (-37°C)	yes	no	somewhat	somewhat	somewhat	somewhat	yes	yes	no
Strawberry *Fragaria* spp.	15°F (-9°C)	somewhat	no	somewhat	no	somewhat	somewhat	no	yes	yes
Thyme, Creeping *Thymus praecox*	15°F (-9°C)	yes	no	somewhat	somewhat	no	somewhat	no	somewhat	yes
Violet, Wild *Viola* spp.	-25°F (-32°C)	somewhat	somewhat	somewhat	somewhat	somewhat	somewhat	yes	yes	yes

yes

somewhat

no

Groundcover	Deer Resistant	Leaf Swallowing	Fast Spreading	Tall	Foliage Interest	Flowering	Wildlife Benefit	Fire-wise	Native Range
Pussytoes *Antennaria* spp.		■		■					North America
Quaker Ladies *Houstonia caerulea*		■		■	■				North America
Ragwort, Golden *Packera aurea*									North America
Raspberry, Creeping *Rubus hayata-koidzumii*								■	Asia
River Oats *Chasmanthium latifolium*	■					■		■	North America
Rosemary, Creeping *Salvia rosmarinus* 'Prostratus'									Europe
Roses, Groundcover *Rosa* spp.	■							■	Europe/Asia
Sedge, Japanese *Carex morrowii*			■		■		■		Asia/Cultivar
Sedge, Pennsylvania *Carex pensylvanica*						■			North America
Solomon's Seal *Polygonatum* spp.									Europe/Asia/North America
Stonecrop *Sedum ternatum*		■		■					North America
Strawberry *Fragaria* spp.	■							■	Europe/Asia/North America
Thyme, Creeping *Thymus praecox*		■		■					Europe/Asia/Africa
Violet, Wild *Viola* spp.				■					Europe/Asia/North America

4 INSTALLING AND MAINTAINING GROUNDCOVERS

While groundcovers are known as low-maintenance, they are not no-maintenance. Nothing is. Groundcovers require a bit of effort to provide them with proper planting conditions to give them a good start. Then, they will need some upkeep during their first few years. After that, they should be fairly maintenance-free. Depending on which plants you choose to use as groundcovers, you may need to touch them only once a year or every few years.

ADDRESSING NEIGHBOR CONCERNS AND LOCAL LAWS/REGULATIONS

Before you strip off your turfgrass lawn, consider the reaction of your neighbors. If they were raised in a culture that prizes a solid swath of turfgrass lawn from sidewalk edge to house foundation, they may find it rather shocking to see your landscape made over into what in their eyes will appear to be a "collection of weeds."

Prepare your neighbors by letting them know your plans to reduce your lawn and your reasons for doing so. Appeal to their love of wildlife or sense of environmental stewardship. Show them that groundcovers can be equally as attractive (or more so!) than a solid turfgrass landscape. Perhaps loaning them a copy of this book will help persuade them?

◀ A modern landscape mixes hardscape materials and low-maintenance groundcovers for an enticing outdoor entertaining area.

Sketch a plan to share with your local homeowner's association (HOA) or government, if turfgrass lawns are required by law or regulation. They may grant you an exception when you present a well-illustrated design with a detailed maintenance schedule to assure them you are not letting your landscape go totally wild.

I find these same tactics work well also with other members of your household who may not be convinced of your lawn renovation plans. Perhaps you can compromise by phasing in the transformation and collaborating with them on your groundcover choices—ranking which ones you all find most appealing.

Most laws governing home landscapes apply only to the front yard, giving you free rein for the side and back yard areas. Laws might mandate a maximum height for any front "vegetation" and that is usually three feet (90 cm), which most groundcovers will easily stay under. Some HOAs dictate a strict list of allowable plants. Try to work within that constraint and find usable turf substitutes within the list. Run for HOA leadership so you can expand the plant list and set looser future regulations.

One way around the lawn police is a gradual transition from all turfgrass to expanding plant beds over several years. This slow expansion is actually a great way to not get overwhelmed yourself as you reduce the size of your lawn and add a new plant bed each year or expand current beds. Broad swaths of green groundcovers, rather than a patchwork approach, may also please those who frown on nonturf lawns.

Even in areas without lawn laws and regulations, you may receive criticism from neighbors who do not welcome change or the see eliminating lawns as shirking your civic duties.

▲ Educational signage helps let neighbors know that a conversion from turfgrass lawn to groundcovers is intentional and deliberate.

To mollify then, keep some turfgrass around the edges of your landscape. It might only be one or two mower-strips wide or something you can maintain with a weed-whacker/string trimmer.

Neat edges go a long way to letting folks know that your landscape choices are deliberate and not signs of neglect. These edges can be hardscaping like a line of bricks or other permanent barrier to contain exuberant groundcovers or they can be very low-growing groundcovers that can take some light foot traffic and then transition to taller/fuller groundcovers as you near your home's foundation.

Place educational signage where passersby can read it. These can help explain your motivation and reasons for your landscape changes. These signs can be home-made, but they carry more authority and gravitas when professionally

▼ Overleaf: This tapestry lawn is a combination of sedums and other low-growing groundcovers to create a pleasing carpet effect.

▲ You may opt to keep a small token amount of turfgrass lawn to appease others and surround it with beds filled with groundcovers and other low-maintenance plantings.

made. Some signs I use in my own landscape include those purchased from nonprofit groups that promote turfgrass replacement and reduce pesticide use. These include "Pollinator Habitat" signage from Pollinator.org, "Pesticide Free Zone," from Beyondpesticides.org, and "Certified Wildlife Habitat" from the National Wildlife Federation, nwf.org—among several others. Your local environmental groups may offer similar signage and certifications in exchange for a nominal donation.

The Tapestry Lawn

A tapestry lawn is one that is a colorful patchwork of different groundcovers knitted together. This term is of recent vintage, but it is not a new concept in gardens and landscapes. Some gardeners create elaborate patterns with their groundcovers that look like living mosaics, murals, or Persian carpets. Others just plant randomly and encourage the various groundcovers to join together and spread as they will.

Not only are they beautiful and practical, but they also benefit the environment and local wildlife. Dr. Lionel Smith, author of *Tapestry Lawns: Freed from Grass and Full of Flowers*, writes, "Tapestry lawns are a new, practically researched and timely development of the ornamental lawn format that integrates both horticultural practice and ecological science and re-determines the potential of a lawn. Mown barely a handful of times a year and with no need for fertilizers or scarifying, tapestry lawns are substantially richer in their diversity of plant and animal life compared to traditional grass-only lawns and see the return of flowers and color to a format from which they are usually purposefully excluded."

The tapestry lawn concept is gaining traction in fashion and design circles. If you encounter resistance to your removal of turfgrass, you might appeal to the aesthetic and trendy nature of your opponents that these tapestry lawns are now "in" and the newest thing in landscapes.

A PATCHWORK QUILT OR SOLID CARPET

A large swath of just one kind of groundcover is pleasing to the eye and makes maintenance simple. Groupings of one species together will make it easier to water at the same time, cut back if it requires early spring attention, catch any weeds that pop up, and to fill in bare spots. This is the method that farmers employ to cultivate crops and conserve resources.

The main drawback of a monoculture of one kind of plant is that if a few are damaged by disease or pests, it spreads quickly from one to another and the whole crop is usually a loss. I witnessed this tragic occurrence first-hand at a friend's home when her Japanese pachysandra (*Pachysandra terminalis*) suffered from a fungal leaf blight. Within a matter of days, the whole patch was defoliated. This plant covered the majority of her front landscape and the impact was quite distressing.

A mix of different groundcovers in the same location is also difficult to achieve. Inevitably, one will dominate the other and takeover. I have seen successful examples of taller groundcovers set in among low-growing ones. Hostas, ferns, and hellebores surrounded by a carpet of creeping Jenny or bugleweed can work, though some thinning and monitoring may be needed.

Spring-blooming bulbs that emerge and die-back by summer also work well for this layered effect. Don't forget about summer-blooming and fall-blooming bulbs as well. Gladiola, allium, or canna can act as vertical exclamation marks in a low-growing bed of carex, sedge, or blue fescue.

▲ Where two different groundcovers meet such as these moss and sedums, they can overlap and transition beautifully.

A patchwork quilt of various groundcovers side by side can be effective and attractive. Each grouping might be a few feet in diameter or several yards wide. The edges of each different groundcover might touch and slightly overlap, but pay attention that one doesn't drown out a neighbor.

Select plants that generally "play well with others," as opposed to those that want to seek world domination. Groundcovers that work well in a quilt-like installation in full sun include lamb's ear, black-eyed Susan, blue fescue, sun-loving sedums, pussytoes, creeping rosemary, and creeping thyme. For shade or part-shade combinations, consider pairing brunnera, miniature hosta, wild ginger, heuchera, and Christmas (or other) fern. Dwarf mondo grass and clumping liriope are nice polite picks for either sun or shade conditions to edge a bed or define an area.

▶ Ribbons of various kinds of hostas run down a steep hillside as a low-maintenance groundcover under a tall canopy of trees.

SPACING AND INTERPLANTING

When starting your groundcover, your choice will be dictated by the various conditions of the planting area. Is it shady or sunny? Wet or dry? Flat or sloped? Once you have chosen the best groundcover variety for your situation. You need to know its eventual spread and mature size. Then you can determine how close to plant them.

Note that there will also be some variation among different cultivars of the same kind of groundcover. For instance, some creeping junipers spread from 3-4 feet (0.9-1.2 m), while others will sprawl out to 8-10 feet (2.4-3 m).

▲ In this example of a matrix planting, a mix of Pennsylvania sedge (*Carex pensylvanica*) is interplanted with allium bulbs. A similar effect can be achieved by adding in tall verbena (*Verbena bonariensis*) among the Pennsylvania sedge or a similar mounding groundcover.

Using the example of creeping junipers that eventually spread to 3-4 feet (0.9-1.2 m), first measure the area you wish to cover. For this hypothetical, we'll say it is 20 feet (6 m) wide and long. You would plant each one at least three feet (90 cm) from its neighbor, so to fill the space, you will need three plants total. There are online calculators provided by groundcover sellers that can assist you with these calculations.

The plants should be placed in a triangle or diamond pattern rather than lined up in a row, unless you are filling in a long, linear border area. There may be some locations in your landscape in which just one, solid groundcover may not be the best solution or you may prefer a mix of plants as a more aesthetically pleasing alternative. In either case, you might use a matrix planting method in which you combine a low-growing groundcover with a higher-growing plant.

In a matrix planting, two or more plants occupy their own root space, but their top growth is overlapping and intermixed. They may emerge and die-back at different times in the growing season. Matrix plantings can be extremely complex, depending on the number of plant choices you include.

To start off, you might choose two plants that mix well together and then experiment with spring-blooming bulbs and annual flowers direct-sown by seeds in any bare spots around them until the matrix fully fills in. In this option, you would not mulch the bare soil or do so very sparingly.

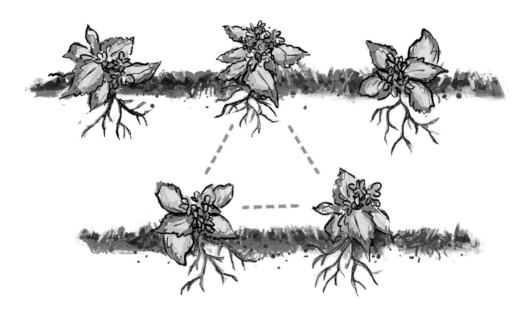

▲ Place groundcover plants in a triangle or diamond pattern for a more interesting and appealing look.

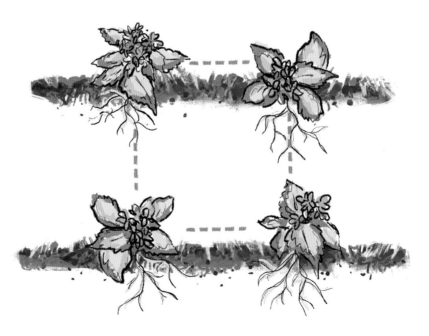

▲ Place groundcover plants in lines or a box where you need to get between them easily to weed or do other maintenance.

▲ Groundcover plants can be interplanted with spring and summer-blooming bulbs. The same method can be used for adding in tall, thin perennials.

▲ Bulbs and groundcovers may be planted at the same time in the same planting holes or layered in between each other.

▶ Lamium is an attractive, flowering groundcover for partly sunny spots in your landscape.

ESTABLISHMENT TAKES TIME

The goal of an established groundcover is to create a solid, healthy root zone that does not allow weeds to germinate or flourish. There will likely be some weeding required as the ground-cover plants get situated and fill in. There is an old garden adage, "First year sleep, second year creep, third year leap." This saying is just as applicable to groundcovers as to any other plant.

The first year it is in the ground a plant is spending its time reviving from transplant shock, getting used to the new growing conditions, and expanding its roots in the new soil. You may not see much growth on top, but growth is happening at the cellular level.

The second year, the plant has started to hit its stride and is testing out its boundaries and situation. It will start putting out tentative growth forays and seeing if those are successful.

You will start to see a bit of growth and increase.

The third year, the plant has got its bearing and is now ready to flourish. You will see a great increase in growth and size. That is why it is best to not move or divide a plant until after its third year, as doing so earlier will reset that three-year adaptation clock. If you do not see a leap in growth during the third year, then reevaluate if the plant needs to be moved to another location where it may do better.

While you wait on this three-year cycle of growth development, fill in any bare areas between your groundcover plants with a light organic mulch. This will help suppress weeds, hold in soil moisture, and insulate the plants' roots from extreme heat and cold. Examples of mulches you might use include composted leaves, pine straw, and shredded bark.

▲ Groundcovers, like all perennial plants, take at least three years from planting to fill out to their mature size.

◄ A newly planted groundcover may look sparse at first, but will soon fill in. In the meantime, keep any exposed soil covered with a light layer of mulch to suppress weeds and hold in moisture.

CLEARING THE AREA

The hardest part of establishing a new ground-cover is clearing out the space and starting with a blank slate. Of course, you could always try planting a new groundcover into an established area, seeing if it will do the hard work for you by fighting for dominance over the weeds. If you have the time and choose an exceptionally aggressive groundcover, this can work. I have experimented with a few groundcovers and found success doing just that with epimedium, lily-of-the-valley, and stonecrop. However, this method requires a large serving of patience and a tolerance for a messy landscape look for several years.

There are several ways to start off with a cleared area when it is a weedy mess or failed turfgrass lawn. Hand-pull all the current planting or cut them off at the soil level. (Set aside any nice selections for transplanting elsewhere.) Cover the area with a thick layer of cardboard or black plastic and wait for everything to die underneath it. Spray a general herbicide. No matter which clearing method you use, it will not get rid of all the weeds, and some may return and need to be re-cut/pulled/sprayed/smothered. I do not recommend any of these techniques. Instead, I favor the layer or lasagna method of creating new planting areas.

To establish a layer/lasagna bed, first cut all the current vegetation down and leave the plant material where it falls. (This is the bottom lasagna layer and it will decay and add nutrients back into the soil.) Next, add a thick layer of newspaper. Be careful to overlap the edges liberally to prevent weeds from reemerging. Have a helper nearby with a hose to wet it down immediately so it doesn't blow away immediately.

▲ Lasagna or layer gardening is a practical way to clear out a weedy area and create a fresh bed for groundcover plantings.

On top of the newspaper, add a thick layer of whatever organic mulch you have available— chopped leaves, wood chips, pine needles, etc. Do this in the fall and let the "lasagna" cook all winter, then plant your groundcover in the newly created bed in the springtime.

Alternatively, you can plant into the lasagna layers immediately. This can be done by cutting through the layers with a sharp knife and inserting your groundcover seedling or plug. You risk the weeds underneath also finding the holes and taking advantage of them, but any future weeding is much less work than weeding the entire bed from scratch.

This works quite well on all areas except steep slopes. If you are dealing with a hillside, then the next best choice is to mow or weed-whack all the plantings down and clear off all the fallen plant material. Then install your groundcover into the hillside and water it in well. You will need to mow/weed-whack regularly around the new plants until they get established and start to spread. Consider terracing steep hills.

STARTING WITH SEEDS, PLUGS OR PLANTS

Groundcovers can be started off by seed, plug, or plants. The best option for each kind of groundcover is dictated by its type and availability. Seeds are the most economical and often give you a wider variety of choices within a species than what is available from commercial growers.

Plugs are seedlings started in small, individual tray cells ready for immediately planting. A tray of plugs is fairly inexpensive and can often be purchased from wholesale growers. You may need to buy a large quantity to meet their order minimum.

Groundcovers sold planted in pots are the most expensive option as you are paying for the time to put into raising a good-sized plant along with the soil, pot, transport, store rental, overhead, and so on. There are some selections that are only available as potted plants and you should factor this into your choice and budget.

▲ This demonstration of various groundcovers shows the diversity in growth rate and coverage among similar plants.

We all want instant results, but gardening teaches us patience. Smaller is better when starting groundcovers. Several small seedlings or plugs will be the same price as a few gallon-sized plants. They will all catch up in a few years and will be the same size plants, ultimately. In addition, it is easier to plant small seedlings than larger ones—especially if you are dealing with compacted soils or working around tree roots.

Sodbusting

If you are starting with a thick turfgrass lawn, removing it is straight-forward. Soak the lawn down to a depth of at least three inches (8 cm) the day before you plan on doing the sod removal or wait to do it until after good, soaking rains. Measure the moisture depth by inserting a screwdriver.

Take a sharp spade and dig down six inches (15 cm) or so. Cut in straight lines and visually square off a piece that is a foot (30 cm) or so wide. Lift up each square section and stack it to the side.

When removing large lawn sections, consider renting or borrowing a sod-cutter machine. Manual sod cutter tools are also available. These will cut just under the turf roots and create neatly sliced strips that you can roll up and apply to thin or bare lawn spots elsewhere, flip it and let it compost in place, or give it away.

PROPAGATION AND FILLING IN HOLES

Groundcovers, like all plants, die. This could be due to damage received in the supply chain before the plant reached the retailer or your garden. It may have started off weak and sickly to begin with. Or it was just naturally a short-lived selection. Whatever the cause, a plant inevitably will die not at the edge of a planting, but right smack in the most highly visible portion of it.

Pull out a dead plant as soon as you see it, in case it is suffering from a pest or disease that might infect the neighboring plantings. Examine it to see if you can determine the cause of its demise to prevent a similar fate happening to the rest of the groundcovers.

You will then need to replace it and fill in the hole that is left. In the plant listings, I share propagation tips for each groundcover. By definition, groundcovers are prolific plants that are adept at reproducing themselves. This can be by reseeding, spreading by surface stems or underground roots, or expanding in clumps.

Collect seed from those that go to flower and entire seedheads to have on hand for when you want to fill in a gap or expand the planting. Label and store the seeds in a glass jar to keep them dry and viable for when you might need them. Golden ragwort and Northern sea oats are two particularly fertile reseeders.

Pry out a section of spreading plants and separate a well-rooted piece to transplant. Some groundcovers are so skilled at spreading by rhizomes that any root piece left in the soil will sprout a new plant. I caution you therefore to make doubly sure before placing these kinds

▲ Inevitably, one area of a planting fails and will need to be filled in with more of the same plant through propagation or division.

of groundcovers in your landscape that this is the location you wish to have them in forever. Later, when you decide to dig out the entire planting (or so you think!), if any tiny root parts remain, it will come roaring back to life. Cranesbill geranium and dwarf comfrey are examples of these industrious spreaders.

Dig and divide clumpers periodically so they don't become too dense and start to die out in the center. Clumping plants are some of the slower groundcovers to fill in and hence some of the more expensive plants to start with. Yet, they are a better choice for those who find spreading and reseeding groundcovers too much work to control their rampant expansion (Also see "Keeping Them in Check" later in this chapter.)

Sourcing Natives

Certain North American native species are difficult to source due to their high-demand, difficulty in starting from seed, and slow growing habits. Trillium (*Trillium* spp.) is one example of this. It takes five to seven years for trilliums to go from seed to first bloom. The cost per plant is prohibitive for establishing a large groundcover grouping from scratch. So, buy a few plants from a reputable plant seller and encourage them to naturalize in a woodland area over several years.

◀ Some plants are extremely slow-growing, such as these Trilliums, which take 7 to 10 years to mature. This can cause them to be more expensive and harder to source.

▲ Irrigation helps a groundcover become established, but should be removed after the first few years.

WATER UNTIL ESTABLISHED

Even if a groundcover is listed as drought-tolerant, it doesn't mean it can survive without any water. This goes especially for native plants that are often described as not needing water to survive. Sure, they might not totally die on you, but you want your groundcover plants to thrive and expand, not barely hang on.

Most new plantings require an inch (2.5 cm) of water during the growing season to get established—more if it is very hot. Keep close track of your local rainfall totals. If you have not had sufficient rain and none is in the imminent forecast, you will need to manually water the new plantings.

Water the root zones not the foliage. Early morning water is optimal as it gives the plants a chance to soak up the moisture before the heat of the day sets in and allows any moisture on the foliage to dry off so as not to cause fungal disease issues.

Hand watering is best, but may be time-consuming. A drip hose with emitters directed at the base of each plant is another fine option. An overhead sprinkler should be your last resort, but if you employ it, monitor it and move it around as needed.

After established, the majority of groundcovers don't need supplemental watering, except in the case of extreme drought. Observe your plants if it has been a few weeks between rain events to see if they are suffering and need extra moisture. You have invested a great deal of time, effort, and expense in them, so don't let them die if you can easily prevent it.

▲ The new spring foliage emerges bright green on *Pachysandra procumbens* amid the old foliage, which is tired and tattered after a long, cold winter. Trim out the old leaves to make room for the new and neaten up the overall appearance.

PRUNING OR CUTTING BACK

Most herbaceous (soft stems and leaves) groundcovers will need to be cut back annually to groom out any aging foliage before the new season of growth starts. Use a weed-whacker, mower, or hedge trimmers to make quick work of it.

If the plants have woody stems, use a sharp pair of pruners to cut out any straying growth and reshape the plant overall, but do not cut too far into the old growth or it may not regenerate.

At any time of year, if you see a dead plant part in your groundcover or a broken stem, cut it out and dispose of it. Be vigilant also looking for signs of pests and diseases; caught early these are almost always easy to treat. Once a whole groundcover bed is infected, your recourse is limited.

"That's the thing about successful groundcovers—they get called bad names when they spread and encroach on other plants. We LOVE them for filling in quickly but when they start going where we don't want them we have to keep them in check."

–SUSAN HARRIS, GardenRant.com

KEEPING THEM IN CHECK

Groundcover plants generally fall in two categories—those that increase by running rhizomes (underground roots) or those that are expanding mounds or clumps. The running kinds are more challenging to control and will need monitoring a few times a year to ensure they stay within bounds.

If you want to stop them from intermingling with neighboring plants, bury a physical barrier at their edge. These barriers can be made of various materials and are sold as "edging" in garden stores and catalogs. Alternatively, maintain the edges periodically between plantings with an edging tool or sharp shovel.

Quick Tip

While you are waiting on an order of groundcovers to arrive or for newly planted groundcovers to fill in, plant annuals from seed to cover the bare soil and prevent erosion, dust, and run-off. Quick germinating and growing selections include alyssum, cosmos, marigolds, and zinnias.

▶ Combine green groundcovers of various textures for a pleasing effect in the garden.

▼ Freshly edged beds separate a lawn area from mixed groundcover plantings of phlox, hellebore, and ferns.

▼ **Overleaf:** Groundcovers line a sunny walkway and fill in under perennials and shrubs.

5 GROUNDCOVER PROFILES

Take the time to explore the groundcover options outlined in this book to find the ideal plant for your situation. This chapter gives you 40+ great options and some suggested cultivars, but there are many more you might evaluate beyond this book using similar criteria and qualifications to those provided here.

In the following groundcover profiles you will find the basic facts about the plants to consider for your groundcover needs. Each profile describes the plant's attributes including any special benefits as well as noting any drawbacks or precautions. The profiles include the plant's ideal growing conditions and care instructions. Most entries share how to propagate them to create additional plants and increase their spread.

KEY TO PLANT ATTRIBUTES

Full Shade	●	Deer Resistant	
Part-Shade/Part-Sun	◑	Leaf Swallowing	
Full Sun	○	Fast Spreading	
Drought-Tolerant		Tall	
Tolerates Soggy Soils		Foliage Interest	
Disease Resistant		Flowering	
Salt Tolerant		Wildlife Benefit	
Clay Tolerant		Fire-wise	
Evergreen			

◀ Grass-like groundcovers are effective and attractive, but much lower maintenance than turfgrass lawns.

Ajuga reptans

BUGLEWEED, CARPETWEED, ST. LAWRENCE PLANT, BUGLE

Bugleweed *Ajuga reptans*

Height	3 inches (8 cm)
Winter hardiness	-35°F (-37°C)
Evergreen	yes; semi-evergreen
Bloom time	spring
Spread speed	fast
Sun exposure	sun to partial shade
Soil type	adaptable; prefer well-draining
Native range	Europe

Bugleweed (*Ajuga reptans*) is a ground-hugging evergreen perennial that spreads by rhizomes that stay close to the surface of the soil. It is a member of the mint family and this fast spreader is considered invasive in parts of North America. The dense mats can choke out weeds and is easily pulled up where it is not wanted. It can tolerate occasional, light foot traffic.

The foliage grows in basal rosettes with small, round leaves. The common variety is a plain, matte green, while selected cultivars have quite attractive foliage in a range of tones and variegation.

Bugleweed blooms in spring with six-inch (15 cm) tall spikes of purple flowers that are visited by flies, bees, moths, and butterflies. The flowers are quite attractive and resemble miniature salvias.

It will tolerate any soil type as long as there is some moisture. Plant it in more sun for heavier flowering, in shade it will still flower, but not as thickly. If your garden is south-facing or the afternoon sun is intense, put bugleweed in a protected spot under a tree to prevent the foliage from scorching.

It is generally pest- and disease-free. It can be affected by powdery mildew or crown rot, but those can be prevented by growing it in the open with good air circulation around it in hot/humid climates.

Bugleweed is a terrific plant for holding banks and slopes in place where you wouldn't want to mow. Plant it at the front of a flower border to fill in around other perennials as well as in containers as a filler.

This is not only a low-maintenance plant, but I'd also consider it practically no-maintenance. There is no pruning or other tasks necessary. The flower spikes die back and disappear quickly on their own, though if you desire to do so earlier, set a mower at the highest height and run the plants over to clear the finished flowers off.

It is easily moved and propagated by taking divisions in spring or fall. Pull a rosette up along with its shallow roots and tuck it in wherever you would like it to get established.

Noteworthy Cultivars

- 'Catlin's Giant' with its taller flower spikes and shiny foliage earned the Royal Horticultural Society's Award of Garden Merit
- 'Bronze Beauty' has bronze-tipped foliage with bright blue flowers
- 'Burgundy Glow' has variegated foliage with splotches of pink and white
- 'Chocolate Chip' has dark foliage with maroon-brown tones resembling a rich chocolate bar
- 'Black Scallop' has shiny, dark plum foliage that contrasts well with lighter green plants

Interesting Tidbit

Bugleweed is also grown for its herbal qualities. It is often mistaken for its close relative gypsywort (*Lycopus europaeus*) and used for the same curative purposes including sleep disorders, weight loss, and to stop bleeding of small cuts.

PUSSYTOES, WOMAN'S TOBACCO, LIFE EVERLASTING

Pussytoes *Antennaria* spp.

Height	3 inches (8 cm)
Winter hardiness	-40°F to -35°F (-40°C to -37°C)
Evergreen	yes, semi-evergreen
Bloom time	late spring
Spread speed	slow to moderate
Sun exposure	sun to partial shade
Soil type	adaptable; prefer well-draining
Native range	North America

Pussytoes (*Antennaria* spp.) is a charming perennial that is native to the eastern United States and Canada. It forms clumps and then can spread into a colony. The flowers are visited by a number of tiny bees and flies.

The basal foliage is a velvety gray-green and the flowers are unique. The flower stalk grows to 6-12 inches (15-30 cm) high and then unfurls to reveal a set of ivory blossoms that resembles a cat's paw when fully flexed.

The foliage stays evergreen in most climates, but in colder ones it will die back and return reliably. It is pest- and disease-resistant. Deer and rabbits ignore it for the most part.

Pussytoes prefer to grow in open woods, on gentle slopes, and in meadows. It is fairly drought-tolerant once established and does not tolerate wet soil conditions.

It does not need fertilizer and actually thrives in lean, nutrient-poor soils. It is a good choice for a rock garden, a gravel garden, or any dry shade situation.

Pussytoes is a low-maintenance plant. Cut off the spent flowers if you do not want it to naturalize and self-seed. It is not a very fast spreader. Divide it in the spring by removing the inner rosettes and moving them out to improve air circulation in the middle of clumps.

It is not a plant that will run roughshod over others and is fairly behaved as groundcovers go. On the other hand, that means weeds and other competition can quickly overrun it, so pull out any potential competitors until it has formed a thick clump.

Noteworthy Cultivars/Varieties

- Rosy Pussytoes (*Antennaria rosea*) are common to the western United States and Canada. Its flower has deep pink bracts with a yellow middle. It is the host plant for the American Lady butterfly (*Vanessa virginiensis*).
- Scented Pussytoes (*Antennaria aromatica*) has foliage that when crushed smells of citronella.

Interesting Tidbit

Pussytoes was used by indigenous peoples of North America as a healing tea for intestinal issues, coughs, and colds. It was even used to treat snakebites. Note that there is no scientific evidence that it is effective for treating any of these conditions.

Asarum canadense

WILD GINGER

Wild Ginger *Asarum canadense*

Height	6 inches (15 cm)
Winter hardiness	-35°F to -30°F (-37°C to -34°C)
Evergreen	no
Bloom time	spring
Spread speed	moderate
Sun exposure	full shade to part shade
Soil type	adaptable; prefer well-draining
Native range	North America

Wild Ginger is a perennial groundcover that inhabits deciduous forests and moist shade areas. It is native to the eastern half of North America. Note that this is not related to the culinary ginger plant (*Zingiber officinale*).

The tiny flowers emerge in spring and hide in the leaf litter under the emerging foliage. Get down on ground level and pull back some leaf litter where your patch of wild ginger grows and you will be rewarded with the sight of these unique flowers. They are said to resemble the color and scent of a decomposing corpse to attract the early-emerging flies that pollinate them. Due to the foul smell, they are not a bloom that you would want to collect and display as an indoor bouquet!

The leaves are why you grow this rewarding groundcover. They are bright green and heart-shaped on short stems. The texture is matte on top and hairy on the underside.

Wild Ginger likes to grow in rich, humusy soils. It prefers moist soil that is well-draining.

It can form a large, thick colony that is dense enough to smother weeds. Divide it by digging up a piece of root section in the spring and transplanting it to a new spot.

It is low-maintenance, deer resistant, and fairly trouble-free. If you notice slug damage (holes in the foliage), sprinkle diatomaceous earth around the plants.

European Wild Ginger (*A. europaeum*) is similar in growth habits to the native *Asarum canadense*, but spreads a bit faster. It has glossier foliage and a more rounded shape. It is evergreen and hardy to -20°F to -15 °F (-29°C to -26°C).

Chinese Wild Ginger (*A. splendens*) is a vigorous, but slower grower, than *Asarum canadense*. It has elongated arrow-shaped leaves with silver streaks and a burgundy underside. It is evergreen and hardy to -10°F to -5 °F (-23°C to -21°C).

Noteworthy Cultivars/Varieties

- 'Eco Medallion' has a silvery sheen to its foliage and is a selection of *A. shuttleworthii*, which is not as cold hardy as the *Asarum canadense*.
- 'Eco Choice' grows denser than the straight *Asarum canadense* species.
- 'Eco Red Giant' grows larger than the *Asarum canadense* species.

Interesting Tidbit

Wild ginger was used by European colonists and Native Americans as a spice by harvesting the root, drying it, then grinding it into a powder—though scientists have detected poisonous compounds in the plant and discourage that use today.

Begonia grandis

HARDY BEGONIA

Hardy Begonia *Begonia grandis*

Height	12-24 inches (30-60 cm)
Winter hardiness	-10°F to -5°F (-23°C to -21°C)
Evergreen	no
Bloom time	late summer
Spread speed	moderate
Sun exposure	full shade to part shade
Soil type	adaptable; prefer well-draining
Native range	Asia

Hardy Begonia is a long-blooming herbaceous perennial that blooms from mid-summer through early fall with delicate pink or white dangling flowers.

Deadhead the blooms to encourage continuous flowering.

The foliage is also attractive with large heart-shaped leaves that are a lovely red on their underside. If you can place the plants in an elevated spot such as along a slope or retaining wall, the sun reflecting through the veined leaves is quite attractive.

It thrives in part sun to full shade with rich, moist (but well-draining) soil. It likes a slightly acidic soil of around a 6.0 pH.

It is a good addition to any woodland garden and it performs well underneath shrubs and trees. It does not tolerate foot traffic, so plant it where people and pets will not trample it.

It will spread to form a small colony if allowed to self-sow. However, if you mulch or clean up around them in the fall, it will prevent them from reproducing. Encourage more seeding by waiting for the triangular seed pods to dry, then crush them up and sprinkle the seeds in the areas you want them to naturalize.

Hardy begonia dies back in winter and re-emerges in spring from an underground tuber. Spread a bit of compost on the soil surface in early spring when the plants are still dormant to give them some extra nutrition; they need little care otherwise.

Begonia grandis has a fairly shallow root system that makes it easy to transplant or divide. That means it does well planted in a tree's root zone. It also lends itself well to tight spaces such as in a rock wall, in the cracks of stone steps, or along a path edging.

It has no serious insect or disease problems. Deer will eat the flowers and can break off and damage the plants during that consumption.

Hardy Begonia is fragrant and attracts pollinators, especially honeybees.

Noteworthy Cultivars/Varieties

- 'Heron's Pirouette' has green leaves and larger pink flowers in big clusters.
- 'Claret Jug' has smaller leaves with blood-red undersides and pink flowers.
- 'Pink Parasol' is a larger, pink-flowered form.
- 'Wildwood Purity' has leaves with a dark backside and large white flowers.

Interesting Tidbit

There are other plants in the begonia family that are more or less hardy, depending on your region. However, most of them are clumpers and not runners, so they don't meet our qualifications as a great groundcover.

Brunnera macrophylla

BRUNNERA, SIBERIAN BUGLOSS, FALSE FORGET-ME-NOT, HEARTLEAF

Brunnera *Brunnera macrophylla*

Height	15 inches (38 cm)
Winter hardiness	-35°F to -30°F (-37°C to -34°C)
Evergreen	no
Bloom time	spring
Spread speed	slow
Sun exposure	full shade to part shade
Soil type	adaptable; prefer well-draining
Native range	Asia

Brunnera (*Brunnera macrophylla*) is a perennial that is in the Borage family. The true-blue flowers are a big clue to that plant relationship.

The dainty blue flowers emerge at the top of long stems in springtime. The flowers are pretty, but the real reason you want this plant in your garden is that it is a tough plant with many positive attributes. In fact, it was named Perennial Plant of the Year in 2012 by the Perennial Plant Association.

This plant's foliage is rough-textured and heart-shaped. The hairy texture of the leaves makes it deer- and rabbit-resistant.

It is a slow-spreading groundcover that expands as a clump. Divide the clump and move sections of it every few years to expand the colony.

The only maintenance needed is a fresh application of organic mulch or compost in early spring and to cut back the spent flowers, unless you want the plant to seed about a bit. Trim off the old leaves if they become ratty or tattered during the growing season.

Brunnera needs to be kept well-watered in its first year, but after that is quite drought-tolerant—making it a good choice for dry shade locations. It is also a great alternative or companion to other shade-loving foliage plants like hostas that are practically deer candy.

The straight species of Brunnera is matte-green, while the newer cultivars have a silver sheen or white variegation to their leaves that makes this plant shine in deep shade.

Brunnera works well on slopes, under shrubs, and in containers.

Noteworthy Cultivars/Varieties

- 'Jack Frost' has a metallic crackle-like finish to its leaves. It is more heat-tolerant than the straight species.
- 'Looking Glass' is a sport of 'Jack Frost' and has a more solid silver leaf surface.
- 'Silver Heart' has bold white frosted leaves.
- 'Variegata' has heavily variegated leaves.
- 'Diane's Gold' has chartreuse-colored foliage.

Interesting Tidbit

The flower sprays of brunnera make an excellent addition to spring bouquets.

Carex morrowii

JAPANESE SEDGE, MORROW'S SEDGE, VARIEGATED SEDGE

Japanese Sedge *Carex morrowii*

Height	12-14 inches (30-36 cm)
Winter hardiness	-15°F (-26°C)
Evergreen	yes
Bloom time	late summer
Spread speed	moderate
Sun exposure	part sun to part shade
Soil type	adaptable; prefer well-draining
Native range	Asia

Japanese Sedge is an attractive, low-growing perennial plant that is evergreen in most regions. It has attractive green blades with variegated coloring depending on the cultivar. The slender foliage moves in the breeze and is lovely combined with bulbs and many other perennials.

It resembles a mophead of ornamental grass or variegated liriope, but in fact it is in a category of plants called sedges or carex. The grass-like blades on it are triangular instead of flat.

Due to these sharp leaf edges, deer leave carex alone and it is also generally pest- and disease-free. Once established, it is quite drought-tolerant.

Japanese sedge prefers moist, but well-drained soil in part-shade. If placed in strong afternoon sun, you may notice the edges of the blades getting a little crispy or bleaching out.

Plant seedlings or plugs in the fall. It is a clump-forming plant that spreads slowly. Divide it in the springtime to propagate new clumps.

The flowers are insignificant. They emerge in late spring on brown flower spikes. Cut them off if you do not like the way they look. They will die back on their own in a matter of weeks.

Japanese sedge is a tough plant and extremely low-maintenance. In early spring, run a hand-rake through it to pull out any spent foliage or cut it back overall by up to a third to renew it. In colder climates, where it is not evergreen, simply weed-whack or mow the foliage down to the ground in late winter.

It is a good choice for holding in a slope or edging a walkway. It can take some light foot traffic and bounce right back.

Noteworthy Cultivars/Varieties

- 'Ice Dance' has attractive green coloring with bright-white edges.
- 'Evergold' has very slender leaves with yellow centers and green edges.
- 'Fisher's Form' has attractive green coloring with creamy-white edges.

Interesting Tidbit

Wholesaler New Moon Nursery in New Jersey writes the following about 'Evergold' carex, "The parentage of this Japanese sedge cultivar is uncertain. It has been speculated that 'Evergold' is a cultivar of *Carex oshimensis*, *Carex morrowii*, or *Carex hachijoensis*." A series of mutations of 'Evergold' called the Evercolor™ Carex cultivars was developed by the Fitzgerald Nurseries in Ireland has developed a series of Evercolor™ Carex. The series includes: 'Everdi', 'Everest', 'Everillo', 'Everlime', 'Everoro', and 'Eversheen'.

Carex pensylvanica

PENNSYLVANIA SEDGE, OAK SEDGE

Pennsylvania Sedge *Carex pensylvanica*

Height	8-12 inches (20-30 cm)
Winter hardiness	-35°F to -30°F (-37°C to -34°C)
Evergreen	somewhat
Bloom time	spring
Spread speed	moderate
Sun exposure	part sun to full shade
Soil type	adaptable; prefer well-draining
Native range	North America

Pennsylvania Sedge is a perennial plant with attractive, narrow, green leaves that turn sandy brown in the autumn. The slender foliage moves freely in the breeze and creates a meadow-like effect when planted en masse.

It spreads by underground rhizomes and forms large colonies. It prefers dry, shade situations and is drought-tolerant.

Deer leave this plant alone and it is also generally pest- and disease-free.

It is native to the eastern United States and Canada where it grows naturally in open woodlands, on slopes, and in upland prairies. It does especially well planted among the roots of oak trees.

Pennsylvania sedge is useful for erosion control, in rain gardens, and in hilly terrain. It is a good solution for an area in the landscape that has variable light conditions as it is fairly adaptable.

Plant seedlings or plugs in the fall. Divide it in the springtime to propagate new clumps.

The flowers emerge on white, feathery spikelets that dry to brown seedheads adding interest and texture.

Pennsylvania sedge is a tough plant and extremely low-maintenance. Weed-whack or mow the foliage down to about 3 inches (8 cm) tall in late winter.

This fine-textured sedge has a soft, weeping appearance. A grouping of it looks like gentle waves in the ocean. It looks good as an underplanting for taller perennials such as ornamental alliums or Brazilian verbena (*Verbena bonariensis*).

Many landscape designers are choosing it as a lawn-substitute for its intense green color and easy care. It can take some light foot traffic and bounce right back.

Interesting Tidbit

Pennsylvania sedge even grows well at the foot of black walnut trees where most plants cannot survive due to the tree's production of a chemical called juglone that kills many sensitive plants.

River Oats *Chasmanthium latifolium*

Height	36 inches (91 cm)
Winter hardiness	-25°F to -20°F (-32°C to -29°C)
Evergreen	somewhat
Bloom time	summer
Spread speed	moderate
Sun exposure	full sun to full shade
Soil type	adaptable; prefer well-draining
Native range	North America

River Oats is an ornamental grass with attractive, long-lasting seedheads. The seeds resemble weeping or drooping grains. The sound of the wind rustling through the plants is pleasing and soothing. You won't be able to resist running your hand through the foliage.

The seedheads are green throughout the summer then dry to a wheat color in the fall. In certain autumn light, they can appear almost coppery in color. Leave it up in winter for its beauty and textural interest.

It is adaptable to most soil types from sand to clay and is very low-maintenance. It needs no supplemental fertilization or mulching. It is one of the few ornamental grasses that does well in shade situations.

It readily self-sows and can form a large colony quickly. Pull or transplant the plants if they pop up where you do not want them to grow. Divide clumps when the flowering slows down or the plants become too crowded.

River oats seedheads provide food to birds and small mammals. Deer also love to browse on them. They are not true oats (*Avena sativa*), though are edible for humans also with proper processing.

It is a good choice for slopes, rain gardens, and erosion control as it develops a firm root mass. Place it where it will not get foot traffic.

Interesting Tidbit

River oats seed stalks are used in flower arranging, especially for autumnal bouquets. They make an excellent dried arrangement on their own in a tall vase.

Noteworthy Cultivars/Varieties

- 'River Mist' has white-striped leaves and the developing seedheads are white.

GREEN AND GOLD, GOLDEN-KNEE, GOLDENSTAR

Green and Gold *Chrysogonum virginianum*

Height	4-6 inches (10-15 cm)
Winter hardiness	-20°F to -15°F (-29°C to -26°C)
Evergreen	semi
Bloom time	spring
Spread speed	slow
Sun exposure	part sun to full shade
Soil type	adaptable; moist, but well-draining
Native range	North America

Green and Gold is a perennial plant with beautiful yellow flowers in spring that forms a low carpet of green foliage rosettes. It continues to flower sporadically throughout the summer. This long bloom period makes it a terrific groundcover for pollinators.

It is native to the woodlands of eastern North America and prefers moist, but well-draining soils. It prefers to be planted in part shade. It can take full sun, if the soil stays evenly moist.

The delicate appearance belies how tough this plant is. It can stand flooding, drought, heat, cold, and the occasional foot traffic. It is virtually pest- and disease-free. Deer mainly ignore it. If slugs or snails eat holes in the leaves, sprinkle the area with iron phosphate pellets.

The growth habit and form is similar to that of strawberry plants. Even the flower itself has some resemblance to that of a strawberry with its open, star-shaped form.

When planting it in clay soils, amend the planting hole a bit with shredded leaf mulch or pine bark. This plant likes to be in slightly acidic ground. If your soil is basic or alkaline, incorporate in some dolomitic limestone.

Propagate it by seed, runners, cuttings, stolons, and division. It actually does best when divided and transplanted every other year in late spring. Snip off the seedheads if you do not want it to self-sow about.

Feed it with a slow-release, organic fertilizer to encourage thick, quicker growth in the spring.

Green and gold does well along streambeds, ponds, and rock gardens. It is a good choice for a rain garden.

Interesting Tidbit

Green and gold is one of the few groundcovers that can be propagated with some success by seed. Collect the nutlets about three weeks after the flowers have faded and dropped. Germination is uneven, but more success has been found when waiting until the soil has reached 70 degrees F (21°C) to plant them.

Noteworthy Cultivars/Varieties

- 'Quinn's Gold' has multicolored flowers that emerge a bright-yellow then turn from light yellow to a creamy white as they age on the plants.
- 'Superstar' has a more prostrate form with shorter flower stems.
- 'Eco Lacquered Spider' has striking purple-colored stolons and glossy leaves.
- 'Pierre' has softer green foliage and flowers prolifically over a long period.
- 'Allen Bush' is a dwarf form with smaller flowers.
- 'Mark Viette' is a slightly taller plant with buttercup yellow flowers.

Convallaria majalis

LILY-OF-THE-VALLEY, MAY BELLS, OUR LADY'S TEARS, MARY'S TEARS, MAYFLOWER

Lily-of-the-Valley *Convallaria majalis*

Height	6-8 inches (15-20 cm)
Winter hardiness	-50°F to -45°F (-46°C to -43°C)
Evergreen	no
Bloom time	late spring
Spread speed	fast
Sun exposure	part sun to full shade
Soil type	adaptable; moist, but well-draining
Native range	Europe/Asia

Lily-of-the-valley is a groundcover that spreads by underground rhizomes (roots). The springtime flowers are held aloft on a stem above the lance-like foliage and the blooms look like a series of little white bells.

The spreading tendencies of this plant are legendary. Keep it in check by planting in a dry, full-shade spot with lean soils. The better the growing conditions you give it, the quicker and farther it will colonize. It easily crowds out any possible weeds that try to pop up in its midst.

Plant the pips (bare roots) or any section of the roots an inch (3 cm) or so beneath the soil level. Keep out of direct afternoon sun, which may burn the foliage.

It is the definition of low-maintenance. At the beginning of spring, I rake out the old, tattered foliage from their beds and sprinkle in some leaf compost. This isn't necessary, but it keeps the bed looking neat.

The scent of the blooms in spring is lemony fresh. To pick some lily-of-the-valley flowers to enjoy indoors, grasp the bloom stem down at the base and then pull firmly upward in one smooth motion.

Note that they are poisonous and should be kept away from small children and pets. Wash your hands after touching any parts of this plant before handling food. It is deer-proof.

Lily-of-the-valley also has fall interest. Leave the flower stems up and they will form seed-containing fruits that resemble orange-red berries.

Interesting Tidbit

There is a version native to North America, *Convallaria majuscula* that is almost impossible to differentiate from the Eurasian import unless they are side by side. The American one is a bit taller and can be found in the Appalachian Mountain woodlands in discrete clumps of just a few plants, rather than in a large patch.

Noteworthy Cultivars/Varieties

- 'Flore Pleno' has double flowers.
- 'Rosea' also known as *C. majalis* var. *rosea* has pink flowers.
- 'Albostriata' has leaves with white-striping.
- 'Berlin Giant' is a taller form.

This tough plant is great for growing under trees and on steep banks or hills. It even grows well under black walnut (*Juglans nigra*) trees. Wherever you have a spot that "nothing can grow" is a good place to try out lily-of-the-valley.

EPIMEDIUM, BARRENWORT, BISHOP'S HAT, FAIRY WINGS

Epimedium *Epimedium* spp.

Height	6 inches (15 cm)
Winter hardiness	-30°F to -20°F (-34°C to -29°C), depending on the species
Evergreen	yes; semi-evergreen
Bloom time	early spring
Spread speed	moderate
Sun exposure	shade to partial shade
Soil type	adaptable; prefer well-draining
Native range	Asia

Epimedium (*Epimedium* spp.) is a semi-evergreen perennial that forms clumps and spreads about a half-foot (15 cm) per year until reaching an eventual mature size of about a yard (90 cm) wide. The blooms resemble sprays of tiny orchids.

Flowers appear in early- to mid-spring and then disappear. In the cold days of autumn, the leaves of many epimedium cultivars take on a beautiful rusty-red hue.

The last few decades have seen an increasing interest in this tough plant and hybridizers have been busy introducing many new selections with mottled and variegated foliage of various shapes, as well as different flower colors and combinations. Be aware that some of the newer selections are not as hardy or suited for groundcover use. (See cultivar box for the most-reliable selections.)

Since the flowers are only around for a few weeks, the leaves are the main focus of this plant. They often have a serrated edge that looks sharp yet is not prickly to the touch. The leaf shape can be narrow like an arrowhead or broad like a small hosta or begonia.

The flowers and foliage appear delicate, but don't let that fool you! This groundcover can run roughshod over other plants such as English ivy. It is particularly great at suppressing weeds and swallowing fallen leaves under large, established trees.

Epimedium does well at the front edge of borders, along pathways, and as a filler plant in between other shade perennials, shrubs, and trees.

It prefers shade and the leaves will develop a crispy, burnt edge if situated in too much sun. They like to have their roots in rich, well-draining soils with plenty of organic matter. However, epimediums are generally very tolerant of nutrient-poor sandy soils or dense clay soils as well. It is an ideal plant for dry shade spots, where many other groundcover plants fail.

This is a very low-maintenance plant. Cut back the tattered foliage in late winter/early spring before new growth begins. This allows for the tiny flowers to emerge and be seen to better advantage.

After about three years in the garden, the plant can be divided and spread around to different spots. This is best done in spring or autumn.

Festuca glauca 'Elijah Blue'

BLUE FESCUE 'ELIJAH BLUE'

Blue Fescue 'Elijah Blue' *Festuca glauca* 'Elijah Blue'

Height	8-12 inches (20-30 cm)
Winter hardiness	-25°F to -20°F (-32°C to -29°C)
Evergreen	yes
Bloom time	summer
Spread speed	moderate
Sun exposure	full sun to part sun
Soil type	adaptable; dry, well-draining
Native range	Europe

Blue Fescue 'Elijah Blue' is a clumping, dwarf ornamental grass with ice-blue foliage. The grass plumes are a tan color and are quite attractive in their own right, but the plant is not really grown for its flowers.

When planted in large groupings, it has a dramatic effect. The finely textured grass blades form a neat mound. Some gardeners like the look of the seedheads left on, while others cut them off. Your choice.

Place it in full sun, planted in the fall to get established before the winter cold sets in. If placed in part-sun, it will survive, but the silvery-blue foliage color will not be as strong.

Plant it in dry-to-average soils that are well-draining. The crown should be right at or just above the soil level so that moisture doesn't collect in the plant and cause rot.

While it thrives in poor soils, when putting on new spring growth it uses up a good deal of nitrogen, so applying a fertilizer high in nitrogen may be beneficial in late spring.

Cut it back in late winter/early spring to encourage new growth. Divide or re-plant it every few years.

These compact plants do not send out runners, so plant them fairly close together for a more full, dense look. Set them a little more than a foot (30 cm) on center from each other.

Blue fescue 'Elijah Blue' is drought-tolerant and is a great choice for hot, dry climates. It does well in rock gardens, gravel gardens, sidewalk edges, and slopes. Due to its salt tolerance, it is also a good choice for coastal regions.

It attracts birds and is deer-resistant. The silver-blue mound is said to resemble a sea urchin or porcupine.

Noteworthy Cultivars/Varieties

Ornamental grasses with a similar blue appearance and growth habit to blue fescue include:

- 'Sapphire' blue oat grass (*Helictotrichon sempervirens* 'Sapphire') like blue fescue prefers full sun and well-draining soils. It grows to two-feet (60 cm) tall with a round, sculpted look.
- 'Blue Zinger' blue sedge (*Carex flacca* 'Blue Zinger') can grow in sun to part sun and likes well-draining soils. Its narrow, grass-like blades form 10-inch (25 cm) clumps. It is a bit more "blue" and less silvery than blue fescue.

Fragaria spp.

STRAWBERRY

Strawberry *Fragaria* spp.

Height	6-12 inches (15-30 cm)
Winter hardiness	-15°F to -10°F (-26°C to -23°C)
Evergreen	yes
Bloom time	late spring/early summer
Spread speed	fast
Sun exposure	full sun to part sun
Soil type	adaptable; moist, well-draining
Native range	Northern Hemisphere

Strawberry plants are a great groundcover with the side benefit of producing delicious, edible fruits. The strawberry flowers themselves are pretty—usually white or light pink.

There are two main kinds of strawberries: ever-bearing and June-bearing. As per their names, ever-bearing and June-bearing make fruits at different times. June-bearing is typically productive from late-May to mid-June, while ever-bearing can have several waves of berries throughout the summer. Select June-bearing if you want one large crop for making jams or freezing. Choose ever-bearing if you want to throw some fresh berries in your cereal bowl every few days.

Strawberries grow best in well-drained soil located in full sun. Mix in plenty of organic materials. Plant out strawberry crown divisions during the early spring. The first year may not yield much of a crop, but the edible fruit is just a side bonus to this groundcover.

Put the new, bare-root plants in so that the crown is just resting at soil level with the roots gentled fanned out beneath the surface.

They need only about one inch (2.5 cm) of water per week and are prone to root rot, so don't overdo it or place them in soggy soils.

Strawberry plants will then send out runners. Cut them off or guide them back into the bed to create a thicker patch. (If more fruit is what you are after, some experts recommend pinching off all the flowers and runners during the first year to get big crops the following year.)

Note that alpine strawberries (*Fragaria alpina*) do not produce runners. It grows in clumps and will need to be dug and divided every year.

Relatively disease-free, compared to other fruits you may grow, they are plagued by a few pests—most notably slugs and birds. To combat slugs, sprinkle iron phosphate around the beds, which is safe for use around edibles. For birds, put some shiny, moving objects nearby. You might also consider investing in screening or bird netting to cover the beds as the fruits ripen.

In the fall, wait for a frost to hit them then mulch the strawberry bed with straw (not hay!) or other materials such as pine needles to insulate the plants over the winter. Covering them before the frost hits and the plants are still warm can result in crown rot. Remove the mulch again in spring.

Strawberry plants also make good border plantings. They stay low and fairly tidy. The runners are easy to pull up if they go astray

It is a fast spreader, but doesn't form a solid enough layer that it outcompetes weeds, therefore you will have to do some maintenance weeding.

Because you are creating a colony of plants and not thinning them as you would in an edible garden, the fruits will be smaller and not as numerous—but still tasty!

Geranium macrorrhizum

CRANESBILL GERANIUM, ALUM ROOT, ALUM BLOOM, CRANESBILL, SPOTTED CRANESBILL, WILD CRANESBILL, SPOTTED GERANIUM, WILD GERANIUM, WOOD GERANIUM, HARDY GERANIUM

Cranesbill Geranium *Geranium macrorrhizum*

Height	6-12 inches (15-30 cm)
Winter hardiness	-25°F to -20°F (-32°C to -29°C)
Evergreen	yes
Bloom time	late spring/early summer
Spread speed	moderate
Sun exposure	full sun to part sun
Soil type	adaptable; dry, well-draining
Native range	Eastern North America

Cranesbill Geranium is also known as hardy geranium and many other names. It should not be confused with the zonal geranium (*Pelargonium zonale*), which is an annual plant with a tall flower spike that is commonly seen in summer window box displays.

The cranesbill geranium spreads by a large underground root system. It's Latin name *Geranium macrorrhizum* (*macro* = large, *rhizum* = root) gives you some indication of how truly large that root is in comparison to the fairly small leaves and flowers you see growing aboveground.

Cranesbill geranium has an exceptionally long blooming period. Sheer back any spent foliage after it finishes flowering to tidy the plant up, if you desire.

Even when not in bloom, the plant is attractive and the foliage itself is fragrant with a rich, spicy scent.

It prefers full sun to light shade and tolerates most soil types. Although it does not like sitting in wet ground and will rot if left for long in soggy soils.

It needs no fertilizing and is fairly drought-tolerant once established but should be watered during prolonged drought periods.

To propagate it, dig up and cut out a section of the root. Plant wherever you would like the geranium to spread.

Cranesbill geranium's flowers are attractive to both butterflies and bees as well as syrphid flies, ants, and beetles.

This is one tough plant. It is disease-resistant and untroubled by insect pests. It is also rabbit- and deer-resistant.

It fills in well in places where many other plants fail, such as under evergreen shrubs and in dry shade. Its dense growing habit makes it a terrific choice to hold a slope, swallow fall leaves, and fight back against encroaching weeds.

Noteworthy Cultivars/Varieties

- Two varieties that have charming, pale pink flowers are 'Biokovo' (a hybrid of *Geranium dalmaticum* and *Geranium macrorrhizum*). It stays fairly low-growing.
- Rozanne® 'Gerwat' is the world's best-selling hardy geranium. It produces large saucer-shaped violet-blue flowers with white centers. It is a clump forming, rather than fast-spreading plant. It is a cousin to *Geranium macrorrhizum* and is a naturally occurring hybrid of *Geranium himalayense* and *Geranium wallichianum* 'Buxton's Variety'.

Interesting Tidbit

There is no need to deadhead cranesbill geranium. In fact, leaving the flowers up to form seedheads has the side benefit of providing food for ground-foraging birds such as mourning doves and quails.

Helleborus spp.

HELLEBORE, LENTEN ROSE, CHRISTMAS ROSE, BEAR'S FOOT, WINTER ROSE

Hellebore *Helleborus* spp.

Height	12-18 inches (30-45 cm)
Winter hardiness	-20°F to -15°F (-29°C to -26°C)
Evergreen	yes
Bloom time	late winter/early spring
Spread speed	moderate
Sun exposure	part sun to full shade
Soil type	alkaline soil; well-draining
Native range	Asia/Europe

There are about 20 species in the *Helleborus* genus. The most common are the Christmas rose (*Helleborus niger*), which blooms in late winter, and the Lenten rose (*Helleborus orientalis*), which blooms in early spring. It is a tough perennial plant that is drought-tolerant and thrives in shade.

It prefers to be planted in humus-rich, alkaline soil with good drainage, but is tolerant of lesser conditions. It is a great choice for planting in the root zone of deciduous trees such as oaks and maples.

When it is happy in a spot, it will seed itself about and soon form a nice colony. If a seedling pops up where you don't want it, pluck it out and move it or compost it.

The large, shiny hellebore foliage is evergreen and resembles short umbrellas, making this a great groundcover for swallowing leaves and shading out competing weeds. The thick, leathery foliage is bitter and distasteful to deer and other creatures like voles and rabbits.

These are very low-maintenance plants. In mid-winter, gently remove any fallen leaves from around the hellebores to be able to enjoy the blooms when they start to emerge in the bleakest months of the year.

Apply a thin layer of leaf mold or composted leaves around the plants to provide nutrition and improve the soil. The only other attention they ever need to do is cut back the old, tattered foliage in early spring, if it bothers you.

Interesting Tidbit

The hellebore is a long-lasting cut flower. The blooms look lovely floating in a bowl of water. I have had them last that way indoors for over a month. It is so nice to be able to enjoy them inside, when bad weather prevents you from going out into the garden.

Noteworthy Cultivars/Varieties

- *Helleborus niger* 'Christmas Carol' is an early bloomer that emerges as a white flower then develops a pretty pink tinge as the flower ages.
- *Helleborus* x *ericsmithii* 'COSEH 710' HGC Pink Frost has gorgeous silver-veined foliage. Burgundy buds open to pale-pink flowers that age to a deep-rose hue. The flower stems are dark-red, adding to this plant's beauty.

The hellebore flower is stunning and the latest breeding introductions are spectacular. Among them are beautiful doubles and blooms with picotee edges.

Because the heavy flowers face down, plant them on a slope so you look up into them or look for newer cultivars with thicker stems that hold the flowers more upright.

Heuchera spp.

HEUCHERA, CORAL BELLS, ALUMROOT

Heuchera *Heuchera* spp.

Height	12-24 inches (30-60 cm)
Winter hardiness	-25°F (-32°C)
Evergreen	yes
Bloom time	summer
Spread speed	slow
Sun exposure	part sun to full shade
Soil type	slightly alkaline soil; well-draining
Native range	North America

Heuchera are native to North America and do well in woodland garden beds, rock gardens, containers, borders, and, of course, as groundcovers. They grow in clumps, slowly expanding over several years.

They are drought-tolerant and prefer soil to be a little more alkaline than acidic. If you have heavy clay soil, then add some lighter gardening soil when transplanting them into the ground.

The only maintenance is to trim back any tattered foliage in early spring and to deadhead the spent bloom stalks (if they bother you).

Heucheras will bloom from early June until the end of summer, but the foliage is the most eye-catching aspect of these perennials. Most varieties do best in part-shade with some morning sun, but there are recent introductions that flourish from full sun to full shade.

One of the most charming aspects of this plant are that the backs of the leaves often have a contrasting hue to the front side of them, so when a breeze blows a pretty secondary color display is revealed.

The flowers are visited by bees, butterflies, and hummingbirds. Heucheras with pink or red flowers have more pollinator visitors than those with white flowers.

For those gardening where there are hot and humid summers, select plants with *Heuchera villosa* in its lineage. *H. villosa* is a species native to the southern Appalachian Mountains. *Villosa* means "hairy leaf" and those fine hairs not only make these heuchera species more

drought-, heat- and humidity-tolerant, but also deer-resistant.

In climates with mild winters, heuchera rootballs can be pushed out of the ground by the constant freeze-thaw-freeze cycle. If this happens, gently push the rootball back into the soil and cover any exposed areas with a layer of composted leaves.

To get more plants, carefully dig and divide the clumps in early spring—make sure that each piece you replant has some good roots attached.

Noteworthy Cultivars/Varieties

Heuchera has seen an explosion of new introductions in the last decade or so, including those with dramatically dark or metallic colors. There are far too many to list them all here, but here are two of my favorites:

- 'Midnight Rose' has almost black veining on purple leaves with red flowers.
- 'Silver Gumdrop' Dolce® has bright pink flowers and glossy leaves with silver veining and a rich burgundy underside.

Interesting Tidbit

Heucheras have been hybridized with another native shade perennial called foamflower (*Tiarella* spp.) to produce the *Heucherella*, which has added even more fantastic colors and textures to this extraordinary line of perennials.

Hosta spp.

HOSTA, PLANTAIN LILY

Hosta *Hosta* spp.

Height	12-24 inches (30-60 cm)
Winter hardiness	-35°F (-37°C)
Evergreen	yes
Bloom time	summer
Spread speed	moderate
Sun exposure	part sun to full shade
Soil type	average to acidic soil; moist, but well-draining
Native range	Asia

Hostas are known for their beautiful foliage that range from bright chartreuse greens to deep blue-green tones. Many hosta plants also have variegated foliage with cream or white edging or patterns.

In addition to their attractive foliage, hostas send up flower stalks of white or purple flowers in the summer that attract various pollinators. Some varieties of hosta are particularly known for their honey-like flower fragrance.

They do best in best in rich, humusy soils that are kept relatively moist, but not water-logged. Hostas prefer shady locations, but can tolerate additional sun exposure with extra watering.

Hostas die back to the ground over winter and leaf back out in the spring, so they pair well with early-spring blooming bulbs like snowdrops or daffodils.

Hostas are very low-maintenance. To encourage more vigorous growth, sprinkle a slow-release fertilizer as they begin to grow in spring and mulch with an organic compost.

If deer, vole, or rabbits are an issue, apply a repellent spray. If slugs or snails chew on the leaves, spread iron phosphate pellets or diatomaceous earth around the plants.

Hostas can be miniature or dwarf-sized with leaves just an inch (2.5 cm) or so wide, all the way up to selections that are several feet wide. There are common hostas that are fairly inexpensive and quite rare ones that cost hundreds of dollars for a single division.

The good thing about hosta is that you can start with just a few as they multiply in clumps and are easy to dig and divide to spread them about and form a dense groundcover in a matter of years.

Interesting Tidbit

Leave the flower spikes up on your hosta plants and you will be rewarded with Cardinals visiting to dine on their favorite delicacy. It is a delight to watch the birds slipping their talons along the stalks, spilling open the seeds onto the ground, and then greedily snapping them up.

Noteworthy Cultivars/Varieties

There are thousands of kinds of hostas and new ones are being introduced all the time. Here are a few tried-and-true ones that are widely available commercially.

- 'Blue Mouse Ears' is a miniature hosta that is fast-spreading. It has round, blue-green leaves that are 2-4 inches (5-10 cm) long.
- 'Whirlwind' is a medium-sized plant that has variegated, twisted leaves with dark green margins. The center colors change throughout the season from bright green to ivory to yellow.
- 'Frances Williams' is a large, mounding plant with heart-shaped leaves that have yellow edges with a puckered texture.

Houstonia caerulea (previously *Hedyotis caerulea*)

QUAKER LADIES, QUAKER BONNETS, AZURE BLUET, BLUETS, INNOCENCE

Quaker Ladies *Houstonia caerulea*

Height	4-6 inches (10-15 cm)
Winter hardiness	-35°F (-37°C)
Evergreen	yes
Bloom time	spring and summer
Spread speed	moderate
Sun exposure	part sun to part shade
Soil type	slightly acidic; moist, but well-draining
Native range	Eastern North America

Quaker Ladies are perennial wildflowers that colonize open woodlands. They put on a beautiful display of pale blue flowers in the springtime and then can re-bloom sporadically for the rest of the growing season.

They self-sow abundantly, but don't mow them before the plants have set seed or you will interrupt that process.

They are also easily transplanted on an overcast day in the fall. Place small clumps of them among stepping stones and along rock walls. Quaker ladies can tolerate light foot traffic.

The basal foliage of Quaker ladies remains at the ground level year-round—even when not in flower.

They do not tolerate competition when they are young, so they should be planted in bare spots and then weeded consistently until they are well-established. Once they fill in, Quaker ladies can ward off further weed intrusions quite well.

They are similar in growth habits and pre-ferred locations to mosses.

Quaker ladies pair well with other flowering perennials or under small shrubs and trees. They act as a living or "green" mulch.

They are also useful for holding in slopes and covering areas too steep to mow.

Quaker ladies are a favorite of pollinators including early-emerging butterflies and short-tongued bees.

Interesting Tidbit

Quaker ladies are often used in herbal remedies and are said to cure a wide range of conditions from freckles to head lice to gout. (As always, check with your physician before using any plant for a medical condition.) The flower petals are also easily plucked, dried, and used in colorful potpourri mixes as gifts.

Noteworthy Cultivars/Varieties

Quaker Ladies relatives include:

- Star violet (*Houstonia pusilla*), is an annual which has a tiny purple flower and occurs in fields from the American Midwest though to the lower East Coast and southern United States.
- Large houstonia (*H. purpurea*), is a taller species growing from 6-16 inches (15-41 cm) high with white or pink flowers. It occurs throughout the American Midwest to the eastern half of the United States.
- Mountain bluets (*H. serpyllifolia*) grow primarily in the Appalachian Mountain range of the United States. It has white flowers with yellow centers.

Hypnum spp.

HYPNUM MOSS, SHEET MOSS, CARPET MOSS

Mosses *Hypnum* spp.

Height	2 inches (5 cm)
Winter hardiness	-35°F (-37°C)
Evergreen	yes
Bloom time	NA
Spread speed	moderate
Sun exposure	part sun to full shade
Soil type	slightly acidic; moist soils
Native range	Worldwide (except Antarctica)

A **moss lawn** is one of the most beautiful groundcover plants you can install. While there is no flowering part to moss, the rich green color and texture more than make up for the lack of blooms.

Moss thrives where many other plants can't, such as in extremely compacted soils or soggy parts of the landscape with poor drainage.

If you find yourself fighting moss in your turfgrass lawn, that is a good indication that the location is much more suitable to be converted to a full moss lawn. (Note: Moss does not kill grass, but moves in where grass dies and leaves an open spot.)

Moss is soft to the touch and can take light foot traffic. Place it among pavers and stepping stones to create a pleasing pattern and effect.

Purchase sheets of hypnum moss and apply them to bare soil in the early spring. Press them in place to ensure a good soil-to-moss contact and keep the area moist, but not overly wet, until the moss becomes established.

Hypnum moss has a good transplant success rate and is highly adaptable to many growing conditions from rock gardens to pathways to tucked near tree trunks.

To deal with weeds that pop up in your moss lawn, dig them by hand and run a mower (or weed-whacker/line trimmer) over them at its lowest setting.

Moss does not tolerate a heavy layer of leaves sitting on it. If your moss lawn is under a deciduous tree, then after all the leaves have fallen, either rake them off or run over them with a mower until they are broken down into very fine pieces that will compost in place.

Deer do not eat moss. In fact, few creatures do as it is so poor in nutrients and the fibrous texture is hard to digest.

Interesting Tidbit

Hypnum moss was formerly used for stuffing in pillows and mattresses. It is still widely used today in crafts, floral arranging, and in terrariums.

Noteworthy Cultivars/Varieties

There are more than 15,000 species of mosses found all over the world in moisture-rich environments. Some other common kinds that make good groundcovers include:

- Cushion moss (*Leucobrynum* spp.) is a clump-forming moss with a gray-green color.
- Rock cap moss (*Dicranum* spp.) is a clump-forming moss with a bright, emerald-green color.

DWARF CRESTED IRIS, LADY'S CALAMUS

Dwarf Crested Iris is a small iris that is beardless and it faces right up at you, unlike so many other woodland flowers that require you to peer at them from a rabbit's vantage point.

The pretty flowers are stemless and come in a range of pale blue, lilac, or lavender with white markings and a narrow, orange or yellow crest on each fall.

Because it grows to just a few inches tall, it is best suited for the borders of woodland paths and tucked in front of shrubs or among tree roots. It does well in rock gardens and on slopes as well.

The plant blooms on the previous year's growth, so it will take a year to establish and flower. The blossoms are visited by bees and hummingbirds.

When not in flower, the narrow foliage is like that of bearded iris, but on a miniature scale and more densely spaced—quickly forming a thick mat that outcompetes weeds.

Like many iris, the rhizome sits slightly exposed above the soil level and should not be fully covered with mulch or other material. This iris can withstand short periods in wet soils, but prefers to be planted in drier conditions.

It spreads slowly by rhizomes. It is easy to divide and share the root divisions or put them in different spots around your own garden. Division is best done in early fall.

To propagate it by seed, allow the seedpods to dry on the plant then break them open over an envelope to collect the seeds.

Dwarf Crested Iris *Iris cristata*

Height	4-6 inches (10-15 cm)
Winter hardiness	-35°F (-37°C)
Evergreen	yes
Bloom time	spring
Spread speed	moderate
Sun exposure	part sun to part shade
Soil type	average to acidic soil; well-draining
Native range	Eastern United States

They are generally trouble-free and require no care once planted. If they are bothered by slugs or snails, sprinkle the area with iron phosphate pellets or diatomaceous earth.

Jasminum nudiflorum

WINTER JASMINE, YINGCHUN (迎春)
"THE FLOWER THAT WELCOMES SPRING" IN CHINESE

Winter Jasmine *Jasminum nudiflorum*

Height	4-6 feet (1.2-1.8 m)
Winter hardiness	-15°F (-26°C)
Evergreen	semi-evergreen
Bloom time	winter
Spread speed	fast
Sun exposure	sun to part shade
Soil type	adaptable, but dislikes wet soils
Native range	Asia

Winter Jasmine is not fragrant, but it is a prolific bloomer when planted in full sun. The flowers appear in late winter and are very welcome in an otherwise barren winter landscape. It also provides sustenance for early emerging pollinators.

This versatile plant is classified as a deciduous perennial, though most consider it a shrub and it can be treated as a vine as well.

Winter jasmine has a weeping habit that is really quite lovely. It is well-suited to cascading over retaining walls and down the sides of steps. It also looks great spilling out of large containers or trained on an arbor or a trellis.

This shrubby groundcover works especially well on a slope or hillside. When planted in the ground, it can sucker and spread. Wherever a bending branch tip contacts the soil, it can form new roots. After snipping off the connection to its "mother plant," these new "baby" plants are easily dug and transplanted elsewhere in the garden or can be potted up to share.

It thrives in a variety of growing situations from full sun to part shade, from wet to dry soils. They are pollution-tolerant and are generally not troubled by pests.

When not in bloom, winter jasmine's stems are lined with small, glossy-green leaves.

Winter jasmine can grow in poor, infertile soils, making it a great choice to quickly cover barren sites and to fight erosion.

This plant thrives on neglect and needs no fertilizing or other regular maintenance. Although, it can form a thicket in just a few years' time. If it becomes overgrown or unruly, prune it back heavily and it will bounce-back well. The best time to prune is in spring, so you don't impact next winter's flowers.

Juniperus horizontalis

CREEPING JUNIPER

Creeping Juniper *Juniperus horizontalis*

Height	4–12 inches (10-30 cm)
Winter hardiness	-30°F (-34°C)
Evergreen	yes
Bloom time	no blooms
Spread speed	slow to moderate
Sun exposure	full sun
Soil type	adaptable; good drainage
Native range	North America

Creeping Juniper is an evergreen, sprawling shrub. Junipers are tough plants. In general, they are deer-resistant, drought-tolerant, and can cope with many soil types.

One plant can spread up to 10 feet (3 m) in diameter, so it is an economical choice if you have a lot of ground to cover. It is not a fast spreader, so it will take a few years to attain its full, mature size. Juniper is not very tolerant of foot traffic on its branches and the new growth can be prickly, so plant it away from pathways and heavily traveled areas.

Junipers are good plants for stabilizing slopes or spilling over a retaining wall. Creeping junipers can be placed in container combinations as well as used in miniature garden railways and rock gardens.

This groundcover prefers to grow in locations with full sun and good drainage. Junipers do not require fertilization. It is best to plant them in spring, so they have the full growing season to get their roots established. That being said, it is very forgiving, even if you plant it later in the year.

Junipers do not respond well to pruning, so plant them in a spot where they can attain their full size without interference. If you notice an occasional dead, broken, or diseased branch, cut it back to the trunk and do not leave a stub sticking out. Clean your pruners carefully after moving to another plant to limit potential disease spread.

These shrubs produce attractive berry-like cones, but junipers are difficult to grow from seed. Take softwood cuttings in early fall to try

Noteworthy Cultivars

- 'Plumosa Compacta' is a nice, full selection that can get 18 inches (45 cm) high and spreads to 8 feet (2.4 m). It is gray-green in the growing season. In winter, the foliage turns a shade of bronze-purple.
- 'Monber' Icee Blue®, has dense silvery-blue foliage that sometimes turns purple in the winter. It grows to 4 to 6 inches (10-15 cm) high and spreads to 6 to 8 feet (1.8-2.4 m).
- 'Wiltonii' also known as blue rug juniper grows to 4 to 6 inches (10-15 cm) high and spreads to 6 to 8 feet (1.8-2.4 m). Its foliage is a striking silvery-blue that has a purplish tinge in winter.
- 'Bar Harbor' grows to 4 to 8 inches (10-20 cm) high and spreads to 6 to 8 feet (1.8-2.4 m). It has dense, blue-green foliage turning a plum color in winter.
- 'Blue Forest' grows to 9 to 12 inches (23-30 cm) high and spreads to 3 to 4 feet (91-121 cm). Its foliage is blue and changes to lavender tones in cold winters.
- 'Emerald Spreader' grows to 6 to 9 inches (15-23 cm) high and spreads to 6 to 10 feet (1.8-3 m). It has bright, true-green foliage throughout the year.
- 'Green Acres' grows to just 4 inches (10 cm) high and spreads to 5 to 10 feet (1.5-3 m). It has thick, dark green foliage.

to propagate additional plants. New growth works best for successfully rooting cuttings.

In late winter or early spring, it is a good idea to clean out any dead leaves stuck inside the plant's branches because junipers like to have good air circulation around them.

If planted in shade, junipers tend to grow spindly and will not fill in well. They also do not tolerate wet feet and can rot in soil that is poorly draining. Junipers planted in shade or in too-wet soils can also suffer from fungal diseases.

Common insect pests affecting junipers include bagworms, spider mites, leaf miner, webworm, scale, and aphids. Most of these can be controlled by catching them in the early stages of an infestation and removing, then disposing of them.

Additional Junipers

Other low-growing and spreading juniper species and varieties that can make great groundcovers include:

- *Juniperus procumbens* 'Nana'
- *Juniperus procumbens* 'Green Mound'
- *Juniperus chinensis* 'Parsonii'
- *Juniperus chinensis* var. *sargentii*
- *Juniperus conferta*
- *Juniperus conferta* 'Blue Pacific'

Lamium maculatum

LAMIUM, DEAD-NETTLE, SPOTTED DEAD NETTLE, GREATER HENBIT, COBBLER'S BENCH

Lamium *Lamium maculatum*

Height	4-8 inches (10-20 cm)
Winter hardiness	-25°F (-32°C)
Evergreen	semi-evergreen
Bloom time	spring-summer
Spread speed	fast
Sun exposure	shade to part shade
Soil type	adaptable, but prefer evenly moist, rich soils
Native range	Europe/Asia/Africa

Lamium has small, snapdragon-like flowers and variegated foliage. It thrives in shade situations and the silver-white streaking on its leaves makes it appear to practically glow in low-light locations.

It does well tucked near shrubs or small trees. It can also be used at the front of a shaded woodland pathway or planting bed.

Lamium pairs well with spring-blooming bulbs as it can cover up their dying foliage and also outcompetes most weeds.

Fertilize lamium when the plant starts expanding in spring and then again in the mid-summer. Spread compost around the plants in fall and again in spring. If your soil is very acidic, amend it with lime.

Shear or pinch back any scraggly or leggy growth in early summer and again in late summer/early fall for a more mounded, compact appearance.

A handful of lamium plants can fill a 40-foot (12 m) area in a year or two. It can be started from seed, but is easiest to propagate by cuttings, stem layering, or division.

Lamium does not tolerate growing in high heat or full sun, so this is not a good choice for very hot climates.

In milder climates, lamium is evergreen. In colder climates, it will die back to the ground and emerge again the following spring. There are annual lamium cousins that are often used in seasonal container plantings, so ensure that you are purchasing the perennial *Lamium maculatum.*

Its flowers attract bees and other pollinators. Lamium is generally ignored by deer and other animals.

Interesting Tidbit

Lamium is in the mint family and like most mint plants it is a prolific and aggressive spreader, which has caused lamium to be labeled as "invasive" in some locations where it is not native. Check your local list of invasive species before planting it and have a plan for how you will control its spread to other garden areas by either installing a physical barrier or doing regular maintenance.

Noteworthy Cultivars/Varieties

- 'Aureum' has light pink flowers with yellow-green foliage.
- 'Beacon Silver' has deep lavender flowers and silvery leaves with a thin green edging.
- 'Pink Pewter' has pink flowers and silver-variegated leaves.
- 'Purple Dragon' has large, purple flowers with small, silver foliage with a wide green edging.
- 'White Nancy' has white blooms with silvery leaves.

LIRIOPE, LILY TURF, MONKEY GRASS

Liriope *Liriope muscari*

Height	12 inches (30 cm)
Winter hardiness	-25°F (-32°C)
Evergreen	evergreen
Bloom time	summer
Spread speed	moderate
Sun exposure	shade to sun
Soil type	adaptable, well-draining soils
Native range	Asia

Liriope is a tough, low-maintenance plant. It is a grass-like perennial that grows to about a foot (30 cm) tall. It is available in solid-colored and variegated foliage versions.

In late summer, they send up pretty spikes of purple or white flowers, which are sometimes followed by attractive dark berries in the fall.

Liriope grow well in many types of soil. It does not like sitting in wet ground for long periods of time and is quite drought-tolerant once established.

It doesn't require any fertilizing. The only maintenance liriope needs is to shear or mow (at the highest setting) it back in late winter or early spring to cut off the last season's fading foliage and make way for fresh leaf growth.

Dig and divide the clumps every few years in the spring or fall, if you wish to spread the plants to other areas of your landscape.

Liriope fills in nicely under shallow-rooted trees and is an acceptable replacement for turf-grass in many communities where lawns are mandated. The grass-like foliage is "steppable" and forgiving of occasional foot traffic.

It is useful for holding in a slope and covering exposed soils as well as for edging a shrub border.

Deer generally do not bother it. It is fairly disease-resistant and untroubled by most garden pests.

Liriope is adaptable and grows well in both sun and shade, making it a great choice for an area or border that spans across different levels of sun exposure.

Interesting Tidbit

There are two main species of liriope. *Liriope spicata* is a fast-spreading plant by underground rhizomes, while *Liriope muscari* is a clumping one. Caution should be exercised before planting *Liriope spicata* as it can be next to impossible to remove it all in future years. Thus, *Liriope spicata* is considered invasive in some areas.

Noteworthy Cultivars/Varieties

- 'Evergreen Giant' has green leaves and white flowers. It grows to 18 to 24 inches high (45-60 cm).
- 'Gold Band' has strappy, green foliage that is edged in yellow with lavender flowers.
- 'Majestic' has large lilac flower spikes and dark green foliage.
- 'Samantha' has green leaves with pink-purple blooms.
- 'Silvery Sunproof' has yellow and white variegated foliage. It is very heat and sun tolerant.

Lysimachia nummularia

CREEPING JENNY, MONEYWORT, GOLDEN CREEPING CHARLIE, HERB TWOPENCE

Creeping Jenny *Lysimachia nummularia*

Height	2-4 inches (5-10 cm)
Winter hardiness	-25°F (-32°C)
Evergreen	yes
Bloom time	summer
Spread speed	moderate
Sun exposure	full sun to part shade
Soil type	moist, well-draining
Native range	Europe

Creeping Jenny is an evergreen perennial with small, rounded leaves on long trailing stems that grow across the surface of the ground taking root wherever a node touches the soil surface. This groundcover creates a true low-growing carpet that is ideal for the front of beds, along walkways, and in damp areas of your landscape.

In summer, upright bright-yellow flowers appear along its stems. The more sun it is in, the better the flowering, but it will even bloom sporadically in part shade. In hot climates, place it out of direct afternoon sun as the foliage can become scorched by the intense rays.

It prefers moist, well-draining locations such as along a streambed, ditch, or where a gutter spills out. It doesn't like to ever completely dry out. This plant loves wet so much that in can also be used in water gardens.

It is very shallow-rooted and it is easy to pull up a section to transplant it. Propagate it by rooting it in water and then planting the sections in damp soil.

Plant it in early spring so that it is well-established by the heat of summer. Space each plant about 18 inches (45 cm) apart and it will fill in quickly.

Creeping Jenny is not troubled by deer or other pests. It is generally disease-free, but can get fungus or rust if sitting for long periods in hot, humid environments.

Like moss, Creeping Jenny doesn't like to be smothered by leaves in the fall, so rake them off to allow the tendrils to get sunlight.

Interesting Tidbit

Creeping Jenny is often confused with creeping Charlie (*Glechoma hederacea*). The latter has leaves with scalloped edges and purple flowers. Creeping Charlie, also known as ground ivy, has a similar growth habit of spreading rhizomes across the soil. If in doubt, squeeze a leaf or stem section and if it smells like mint, it is creeping Charlie.

It can tolerate light foot traffic and is extremely low-maintenance. It needs no fertilizer or annual pruning, simple cut out any dead or wandering stems as you notice them.

Noteworthy Cultivars/Varieties

- 'Goldilocks' has shiny, golden foliage.
- 'Aurea' has chartreuse green leaves that turn bright-yellow in high amounts of sunlight.

Ophiopogon japonicus 'Nanus'

DWARF MONDO GRASS, MONKEY GRASS, DWARF LILYTURF

Dwarf Mondo Grass is a lush, mounding plant that forms a low groundcover. The deep blue-green color is pleasing to the eye and contrasts well with many other landscape plantings.

It can take some light foot traffic, so does well planted in-between stepping stones or pavers, along pathway edges, and at the fronts of garden beds as a neat border.

Mondo grass holds in slopes successfully and also thrives in rock garden settings. It is also popular as a groundcover in Asian-themed and miniature gardens.

It does best in part-sun to part-shade. If planted in full sun, water it more often and cut off any tips that get sun-scalded.

Dwarf mondo grass is generally trouble-free, though if it sits for long periods in wet soils, it can suffer from root rot. It is deer-resistant and quite salt-tolerant. It is also fairly drought-tolerant and can be planted in the root zone of black walnut trees.

In very cold winters, some blades on the mondo grass can turn brown and a bit ragged looking. Simply run a lawnmower or string-trimmer over it in late winter or early spring. Be careful though not to cut into the crown of the plants as that can injure the newly emerging growth.

To establish a solid groundcover area, plant dwarf mondo grass about 4 to 6 inches (10-15 cm) apart in a grid-like pattern.

Lift and divide dwarf mondo grass every few years to fill in any bare spots and create a fuller look. Use a sharp hatchet or garden knife to separate the clumps if they are root-bound or growing tightly together.

Dwarf Mondo Grass *Ophiopogon japonicus* 'Nanus'

Height	4-6 inches (10-15 cm)
Winter hardiness	-5°F (-20°C)
Evergreen	evergreen
Bloom time	summer
Spread speed	moderate
Sun exposure	part sun to part shade
Soil type	adaptable, well-draining soils
Native range	Asia

Interesting Tidbit

Dwarf mondo grass is often mistaken for liriope, but mondo grass is generally shorter, more compact, and has a narrower leaf blade. The berries on mondo grass are a metallic blue versus the larger black berries on liriope.

Noteworthy Cultivars/Varieties

- `Silver Mist' is a variegated form with green-and-white foliage.
- Black mondo grass (*Ophiopogon japonicus* 'Nigrescens') has very dark green foliage that appears almost black.

Dwarf mondo grass does put out a small spike of flowers in the summer, but the blooms are fairly insignificant and go unnoticed among the strappy foliage.

Opuntia spp.

PRICKLY-PEAR, OPUNTIA, PEAR CACTUS, BEAVER TAIL PEAR

Prickly Pear *Opuntia* spp.

Height	1-5 feet (30-150 cm)
Winter hardiness	-25°F (-32°C)
Evergreen	evergreen
Bloom time	summer
Spread speed	slow
Sun exposure	sun
Soil type	adaptable, well-draining soils
Native range	North America

Prickly Pear is a fun plant to grow that is a great conversation piece in the garden. They are not "steppable," which makes them a good choice for locations where you want to discourage foot traffic.

The Eastern prickly pear cactus (*Opuntia humifusa* or *Opuntia compressa*) is the only hardy cactus native to the Mid-Atlantic United States. It is closely related to the fragile prickly-pear (*Opuntia fragilis*) from the USA's Great Plains and Drummond's prickly-pear (*Opuntia pusilla*), occurring in the southeastern United States as well as a number of other *Opuntia* varieties found throughout Central and South American and the Caribbean. It was introduced to Australia in the last century and is now considered invasive there.

It prefers rocky or sandy soil with good drainage. Plant it along a sidewalk edge, slope, or retaining wall. It also grows well in containers.

Like all cacti, it needs full sun and to be kept relatively dry.

Prickly pear forms clumps and spread relatively slowly. It can be propagated by seed or by breaking off a pad, letting the cut dry for a few days, then sticking it in the soil cutting-side down.

The plant survives freezing temperatures just fine, though it may look a little sad when it dehydrates, lies flat, and wrinkles up during the winter months.

Wear thick gloves whenever handling any part of the plant. The brown bristles and spines are easy to see and avoid, but the fruits are also

Interesting Tidbit

The plant commonly has beautiful yellow flowers in early summer, which then form red fruits (also known as the pears or tunas). Prickly pear fruit is edible as are the cactus' paddles also called nopales. The flower petals can also be added to a salad for a delicious color accent.

Noteworthy Cultivars/Varieties

- *Opuntia* x *basilaris* 'Baby Rita' is a dwarf hybrid with lipstick-red colored flowers and paddles that have purplish skin.
- Spineless prickly pear (*Opuntia cacanapa* or *Opuntia ellisiana*) are not cold hardy to winters that go below 0 degrees F (-15°C) and are hard to propagate, so are best used as an indoor houseplant.

covered in small, hair-like prickles (glochids) that can get under your skin like splinters.

It also a beneficial plant for a number of pollinators and the fruit is consumed by various wildlife.

Pachysandra procumbens

PACHYSANDRA, ALLEGHENY SPURGE, MOUNTAIN PACHYSANDRA

Pachysandra *Pachysandra procumbens*

Height	6-10 inches (15-25 cm)
Winter hardiness	-25°F (-32°C)
Evergreen	evergreen
Bloom time	late spring to early summer
Spread speed	slow
Sun exposure	shade to part sun
Soil type	moist, humusy, acidic soils
Native range	North America

Pachysandra procumbens has attractive green foliage with a light pattern of silver veining.

In warmer climates, the leaves and stems are evergreen. In late spring to early summer, it has fragrant, white flower spikes.

It does best in woodland conditions. Avoid planting it in full sun or poorly draining soils.

Once established, this plant is deer-resistant, disease-resistant, and fairly drought-tolerant.

It spreads slowly into colonies via long rhizomes. *Pachysandra procumbens* is a good choice for shady slopes as an erosion control plant.

The leaves are held up toward the top of the stems, shading out weeds below and also swallowing up fallen leaves efficiently. It is the perfect plant to grow below a large deciduous tree to act as a living, green mulch around it.

To establish an area, group three to four plants per square foot (0.9 sq. m), spacing them a half-foot to a foot (15-30 cm) apart. Do not overwater. Soak the area every two weeks or so, if needed.

Until the plants fill in, mulch between them with an organic compost of partially composted leaves or pine needles, to prevent weeds. You do not need to add more mulch once the plants have filled in.

The only other maintenance required is to remove any yellow or dead growth with a hand pruner throughout the growing season. If there is a lot of winter die-back, mow over them at a high height setting to rejuvenate the bed for the upcoming growing season.

Interesting Tidbit

In comparison to Japanese spurge (*Pachysandra terminalis*), *Pachysandra procumbens* is much slower to fill in and significantly less aggressive. While it may take a few years longer to create a solid groundcover area, it is worth the wait to not have to deal with decades of maintenance to keep it in check as is the case with Japanese spurge.

Noteworthy Cultivars/Varieties

- *Pachysandra procumbens* 'Pixie' is a dwarf version of the straight species that grows to only 4 inches (10 cm) in height and forms clumps.
- *Pachysandra procumbens* 'Eco Treasure' has more variegated foliage coloring than the straight species.

Packera aurea

GOLDEN RAGWORT, PACKERA, SENECIO, GOLDEN GROUNDSEL, BUTTERWEED, FALSE VALERIAN, COUGH WEED

Golden Ragwort *Packera aurea*

Height	12-24 inches (30-60 cm)
Winter hardiness	-35°F (-37°C)
Evergreen	evergreen
Bloom time	spring
Spread speed	moderate
Sun exposure	shade to part sun
Soil type	moist, humusy, acidic soils
Native range	North America

Golden Ragwort has bright-green, glossy foliage that hugs the ground and stays evergreen in mild climates. In the spring, it sends up stems between a foot or two (30-60 cm) high that have black buds at the tip. These buds soon open to reveal golden-yellow, daisy-like flowers that last for several weeks.

The basal foliage spreads along the ground and forms a dense groundcover. It will naturalize in moist areas and self-sow around the garden, if you let it. To curtail that, get out your pruners and deadhead the flowers at the base once the blooms are finished, although part of this plant's charms are the puffs of spent flowers and its seedheads.

While it prefers moist soils, it will tolerate drier conditions as well as occasional flooding.

Golden ragwort is adaptable to many situations, making it a great groundcover for an area of the landscape that ranges in sun exposure. It looks good in a shady border or around the margins of a pond. It does equally well in a sunny or shady perennial bed, as long as it receives adequate moisture.

Divide golden ragwort in the spring. Other than that, it is maintenance-free.

The flowers are attractive to bees and butterflies.

Like most aster family members, golden ragwort is deer- and rabbit-resistant. It is untroubled by most pests and is practically disease-free.

Interesting Tidbit

Golden ragwort (*Packera aurea*) was formerly known as *Senecio aureus*. According to plant expert Barry Glick, "It, along with several other *Senecio* species, was found to have different morphological characteristics and chromosome numbers, so it was given its own genus, *Packera*, in honor of Canadian botanist John G. Packer of the University of Alberta, who has done extensive work with this group of plants."

Noteworthy Cultivars/Varieties

- *Packera aurea* 'Dark Shadows' has deep-purple coloring on the newly emerging spring leaves and flower buds.
- *Packera aurea* var. *gracilis* is shorter and more compact than the straight species with much smaller basal leaves. It also tolerates drier conditions and is more clump-forming than the straight version.

Phlox stolonifera

CREEPING PHLOX, STAR ROCK PHLOX, WOODLAND PHLOX, TUFTED CREEPING PHLOX

Creeping Phlox *Phlox stolonifera*

Height	6-8 inches (15-20 cm)
Winter hardiness	-15°F (-26°C)
Evergreen	evergreen
Bloom time	spring
Spread speed	moderate
Sun exposure	full sun to part shade
Soil type	well-draining
Native range	North America

Creeping Phlox is a groundcover that resembles a thick green carpet. When in bloom, it is sprinkled with purple, blue, pink, or white flowers.

For best flowering, give it full to part sun and shear or pinch back the blooms after the first flowering for a secondary bloom show later in the season. It can take some shade, though the flowering will be less prolific.

Plant it between pavers and along pathways. It can take moderate foot traffic and bounce right back.

It adapts well to various soil conditions. It looks great hugging a gentle slope for erosion control.

Creeping phlox does not tolerate sitting in wet soils for long periods or having organic material like leaves or mulch sitting on top of it.

It should be kept well-watered for its first year, it is quite drought-tolerant after that.

It spreads by surface stems (stolons) that root at the growth nodes to form a solid groundcover. It is easy to propagate creeping phlox by cutting stem sections of 4 to 6 inches (10-15 cm) long from the parent plant during the late summer or early fall. Treat the bottom end of the cutting with a rooting hormone to help it along and plant it in a well-drained, soil-less growing medium.

It is deer- and rabbit-resistant. The fragrant flowers attract many pollinators and it is a butterfly favorite.

Interesting Tidbit

A close relative of *Phlox stolonifera* is *Phlox subulata*, which is also known as creeping phlox, moss phlox, moss pink, or mountain phlox. It forms thick moss-like mats of needle-like, yet soft to the touch, foliage.

Another relative is woodland phlox (*Phlox divaricata*), which grows a bit taller and has a less dense spreading habit. It prefers afternoon shade and a bit more moisture than *Phlox stolonifera*.

Noteworthy Cultivars/Varieties

- 'Sherwood Purple' has lilac flowers and is a vigorous grower.
- 'Fran's Purple' is similar in color to 'Sherwood Purple', but is shorter with smaller leaves. It was also rated a top performer in the Mt. Cuba Center phlox trials.
- 'Blue Ridge' has light-blue flowers.
- 'Home Fires' has bright-pink flowers.

Polygonatum spp.

SOLOMON'S SEAL, KING SOLOMON'S SEAL

Solomon's Seal *Polygonatum* spp.

Height	1-3 feet (30-90 cm)
Winter hardiness	-35°F (-37°C)
Evergreen	no
Bloom time	spring
Spread speed	moderate
Sun exposure	full to part shade
Soil type	moist, well-draining
Native range	North America/Europe/Asia

Solomon's Seal is a lovely perennial with gracefully arching stems. The bell-shaped blossoms dangle along the stems below the foliage in mid-spring to late spring. The flowers last for several weeks and then turn into fruits that are enjoyed by birds.

It prefers moist, well-draining soil that is amended with organic compost or fallen leaves. They are drought-tolerant once established and can do well competing with the roots of nearby trees and shrubs, so it makes a good understory groundcover.

It spreads by underground rhizome. It takes its time getting rooted the first year or two, then it will take off like a rocket in subsequent years.

If it spreads to unwanted areas, dig and divide the plants. It is easy to move it by pulling up a root section in spring. Plant a piece of the root a few inches deep and keep it well-watered that first season.

Solomon's seal is not evergreen. It goes dormant in the wintertime but does not require any deadheading or cleaning up. It combines well with spring-flowering bulbs like daffodils and tulips. As those bulbs die-back in spring, the Solomon's seal foliage emerges and covers up those fading plants.

There is a dwarf version that is 6 to 8 inches (15-20 cm) high as well as tall one that is over 6 feet (1.8 m) high. The common garden varieties are typically between 1 to 3 feet (30-91 cm) tall. There are solid green kinds as well as many variegated ones. The variegated ones are

especially attractive in deep shade portions of the landscape where they can add a bit of light and drama.

Polystichum acrostichoides

CHRISTMAS FERN

Christmas Fern *Polystichum acrostichoides*

Height	1-2 feet (30-60 cm)
Winter hardiness	-35°F (-37°C)
Evergreen	yes
Bloom time	spring
Spread speed	slow
Sun exposure	full to part shade
Soil type	moist, well-draining
Native range	North America

The **Christmas Fern** can have many garden uses from edging plants to groundcovers and even featured in containers.

Ferns in general are extremely low-care. It is deer-proof and has few pests.

It thrives in consistently moist, well-draining soils with lightly dappled to full shade. Water it consistently the first year to get it established and it will be fairly drought-tolerant after that. Most ferns also appreciate a top-dressing of composted leaves.

Colonies of fern can spread and clumps expand over time. They are fairly easy to dig and divide in spring once the new growth (those adorable fiddleheads!) have emerged.

Christmas fern is evergreen in most regions. Reportedly the photosynthesis cycle of this fern continues into the winter. Although the individual fronds do not stay on forever, the old fronds wither away when the new ones come out. If they bother you, cut the old ones to the ground as they will look a bit ratty and tattered in late winter or leave them alone as they disappear soon enough on their own.

Christmas fern reproduces by spores. It can colonize a cleared woodland area and is excellent for holding the soil on shady slopes and hillsides. Ground-nesting birds appreciate the coverage that these leathery-leafed plants provide.

The long-lasting fronds of the Christmas fern are also useful in cut-flower arrangements and in holiday décor. It was used extensively for wreath-making before plastic decorations became the norm.

Interesting Tidbit

This fern gets its name as the individual leaflets (pinnae in fern terminology) that run along the stem—going from smaller to larger—have a boot-like lobe at the top, giving them a Christmas stocking outline. (Some say it is more like a winter mitten!)

Noteworthy Cultivars/Varieties

There are many other hardy ferns, those ferns that are perennial to your growing region, that can make excellent groundcover choices. Two terrific ferns to consider are the bright, yellow-green fronds of the ostrich fern (*Matteuccia struthiopteris*) or the Japanese painted fern (*Athyrium niponicum* var. *pictum*), which practically glows with its silvery highlights. Try a few kinds in different spots. Warning! Fern collecting can be addictive, you may find it hard to stop.

Rosa spp.

GROUNDCOVER ROSES, CARPET ROSES, CREEPING ROSES

Groundcover Roses *Rosa* spp.

Height	1-3 feet (30-91 cm)
Winter hardiness	-20°F (-30°C)
Evergreen	somewhat
Bloom time	spring-fall
Spread speed	slow
Sun exposure	full to part sun
Soil type	well-draining
Native range	Europe/Asia

Groundcover Roses are roses with a spreading or trailing growth habit making them appropriate for groundcover uses.

The roses used for groundcovers are generally low-growing and widely sprawling. They form thick colonies that can scramble down sunny hillsides and slopes.

Plant them in full sun for the best flower production, but they can do well in lower-light conditions too.

Groundcover roses are bred to be disease-resistant and low-maintenance. Cut back the roses by two-thirds in late winter/early spring to encourage full, dense plants with lots of blooms.

They do not form a dense mat of foliage so weeds can pop up underneath them. Add an organic fertilizer around the plants' base and spread a thick layer of wood chip mulch in spring. Mulch again in late fall if you are in a cold region to insulate the plants.

They may spread by a branch touching the soil and developing roots to form a new plant.

They can also be propagated by stem cuttings. Although it is illegal to do so with plants that are patented.

Groundcover roses can bloom on and off for months at a time. Most are self-cleaning and do not need deadheading.

Occasionally, a groundcover rose will throw out a branch that grows straight up or at an odd angle. Prune whenever you notice that happening.

Like all roses, they are susceptible to pests and specific issues. Keep an eye out for rose rosette, rose aphids, sawfly larvae, black spot, powdery mildew, and rose rust. Treat them as soon as you are able.

Interesting Tidbit

Groundcover roses have thorns—although typically not as large as some roses—they can still scratch. That makes them a good choice for an area where you want to keep out trespassers and act as a security barrier.

Noteworthy Cultivars/Varieties

- Apricot Drift® has double apricot blooms and grows to only 1.5 feet (46 cm) high, making it a good choice for along pathways.
- Flower Carpet® Pink has clusters of pink blooms with white centers.
- Playful Happy Trails™ has an open face with red petals surrounding a bright-yellow eye and stamens.
- Oso Easy® Fragrant Spreader has single lilac-pink blooms with a white center.

Salvia rosmarinus 'Prostratus' and *Thymus praecox*

CREEPING ROSEMARY AND CREEPING THYME

Creeping Rosemary, Prostrate Rosemary *Salvia rosmarinus* 'Prostratus' (formerly *Rosmarinus officinalis* 'Prostratus')

Height	1-2 feet (30-60 cm)
Winter hardiness	15°F (-9°C)
Evergreen	yes
Bloom time	spring-fall
Spread speed	slow
Sun exposure	full to part sun
Soil type	well-draining
Native range	Europe

Creeping Rosemary is a low-growing shrub that spreads along the ground forming a thick mat of foliage.

Tiny, pale-blue flowers appear in sprinkles across the plant from spring through fall. This groundcover even emits a rich fragrance when anyone brushes against it.

Creeping rosemary prefers sandy, rocky soils that are well-draining. It cannot tolerate sitting in wet conditions for long.

Plant it on a slope, along sunny pathways, or around/under open-growing plants such as shrub roses.

No maintenance is required except to prune it back wherever you do not want it to grow. Use those cuttings as you would any rosemary for cooking or other herbal preparations.

Creeping rosemary attracts various pollinators such as hummingbirds and butterflies, but is not palatable to deer and rabbits due to its fragrant oils.

Creeping Thyme, Mother of Thyme, Wild Thyme, Wholly Thyme *Thymus praecox* and *T. serpyllum*

Creeping Thyme is an extremely low-growing perennial herb that forms a thick carpet of foliage. The foliage may turn a bronzy-burgundy color in winter.

This groundcover is "steppable" and can be planted among pavers and along sunny pathways. It gives off a delicious fragrance when trod upon.

It is covered in tiny, pink-purple flowers that attract butterflies. It is deer- and rabbit-resistant.

It prefers sandy, rocky soils that are well-draining and cannot tolerate sitting in wet conditions.

Cut it back when it looks a bit scruffy to keep it tidy, as desired.

Propagate it by taking semi-hardwood cuttings in late summer or dig and divide a section.

Mulch is essential in winter for cold climates. During extreme cold, add extra cover protection.

Height	3 inches (8 cm)
Winter hardiness	15°F (-9°C)
Evergreen	yes
Bloom time	spring-fall
Spread speed	moderate
Sun exposure	full to part sun
Soil type	well-draining
Native range	Europe/Asia/Africa

Noteworthy Cultivars/Varieties

- 'Elfin' is a cultivar that has tiny leaves and is slow-growing.
- 'Highland Cream' has green leaves with creamy white edges and lavender blooms.
- 'Pink Chintz' has fuzzy, deep-green foliage with pink flowers.

Rubus hayata-koidzumii (formerly *Rubus calycinoides* and *R. rolfei*)

CREEPING RASPBERRY, FORMOSAN CARPET RASPBERRY, CRINKLE-LEAF CREEPER, TAIWANESE CREEPING RUBUS, CREEPING BRAMBLE

Creeping Raspberry *Rubus hayata-koidzumii* (formerly *Rubus calycinoides*)

Height	6-12 inches (15-30 cm)
Winter hardiness	-5°F (-20°C)
Evergreen	yes
Bloom time	summer
Spread speed	slow
Sun exposure	full to part sun
Soil type	well-draining
Native range	Asia

Creeping Raspberry is a low-growing raspberry relative that is a member of the rose family. The attractive leaves are held on cane-like stems that form a dense mat on the ground. It does well on slopes as an erosion control.

It has white flowers in early summer that turn into edible fruits that are golden in color—similar in shape to blackberries or other raspberries.

For best fruiting, plant it in full sun. However, the leaves can be scorched in intense afternoon sun, so place it where it can get a bit of shade late in the day in hotter climates.

The leaves turn a rust color in fall and, in most regions, stay on over the winter. In some colder climates, it is semi-evergreen, but root-hardy.

One plant can spread 4 to 6 feet (1.2-1.8 m) in diameter. If it goes beyond its bounds, prune it back at any time. Trim out any dead or broken cane stems whenever you notice them.

There are some "soft" thorns along the canes and they are not usually a problem. Avoid stepping on it though, due to these thorns and the stiff canes/stems that can break when trod upon.

If you are in a cold climate, give it extra mulch in late fall for winter protection. Fertilizer is not necessary, but a top dressing of organic compost in early spring can be beneficial and encourage fruit production as well. No need to rake up any fallen leaves in autumn as they also add to the plant's nutrients.

Take cuttings in the early summer to prop-agate it or harvest seeds from ripened fruits. Plant the seeds soon after harvesting.

It is not generally troubled by pests. Birds may eat the fruits, but deer generally leave this tough plant alone.

Overwatering may cause root rot in wet or heavy soil and good drainage is a must. It is drought-tolerant once established.

Noteworthy Cultivars/Varieties

- 'Emerald Carpet' has deep-green, heavily textured leaves.
- 'Golden Quilt' has new foliage growth in spring that emerges bright-yellow and then turns green in summer and red in fall.

Interesting Tidbit

Sterilize your tools between pruning this and other rose family relatives so that you do not transmit diseases among them. A good garden hygiene practice is to swipe the pruner blades with an alcohol swab after each cut. Be careful to not cut yourself and wear leather gloves whenever pruning.

Rudbeckia spp.

BLACK-EYED SUSAN, GOLDEN CONEFLOWER, ORANGE CONEFLOWER, GLORIOSA DAISY, YELLOW OX-EYE DAISY, BROWN-EYED SUSAN, YELLOW DAISY, BROWN BETTY

Black-Eyed Susan *Rudbeckia* spp.

Height	1-2 feet (30-60 cm)
Winter hardiness	-25°F (-32°C)
Evergreen	no
Bloom time	summer
Spread speed	moderate
Sun exposure	full to part sun
Soil type	well-draining
Native range	North America

Black-Eyed Susan is a native North American wildflower. The plant forms clumps of coarse, green basal foliage that spread by rhizomes creating a thick mat of along the ground choking out any competing weeds.

It has one of the longest bloom periods of any garden perennial and can flower from July through September and beyond. Deadheading will extend the bloom time by encouraging the plant to send up more flowers after the first flush. Rudbeckia is an excellent cut flower and can be used dried in arrangements as well.

It prefers full sun, but can thrive and flower in part-sun situations. It is quite hardy and drought-tolerant, once established, and is not picky about soil types. There is no need to add any artificial fertilizer to it, instead I give them a thin layer of organic compost each spring.

Rudbeckia form clumps and can spread by runners or by reseeding. It grows to about 2 to 3 feet (60-91 cm) wide by about as high.

Black-eyed Susans are easy to dig and divide to fill in bare spots. The best time to do so is in the early fall, with mid-spring being a secondary option.

Butterflies and other pollinators are big fans of this flowering groundcover. Leave the seed-heads up for winter garden interest and to feed the birds.

Interesting Tidbit

The black-eyed Susan has many species in the *Rudbeckia* family. They can range from dwarf-sized to quite tall (such as *Rudbeckia laciniata* which is also known as the outhouse plant or the green-headed coneflower). Some are very short-lived perennials or are annuals that will reseed. Be sure of the kind you are selecting by looking at the Latin name. Good choices for long-lasting groundcover use are the *Rudbeckia hirta* and *Rudbeckia fulgida* cultivars.

Noteworthy Cultivars/Varieties

- *Rudbeckia hirta* 'Autumn Colors' has dark-orange to red flowers.
- *Rudbeckia fulgida* 'Goldsturm' has a classic yellow daisy look with a deep-brown center.
- *Rudbeckia hirta* 'Sonora' has large yellow flowers with a burgundy inner ring and dark-brown center.
- *Rudbeckia hirta* 'Toto' is a shorter selection good for the front of borders and along walkways.

Sedum ternatum

STONECROP, WILD STONECROP, WOODLAND STONECROP, THREE-LEAVED STONECROP, WHORLED STONECROP

Stonecrop *Sedum ternatum*

Height	2-5 inches (5-13 cm)
Winter hardiness	-35°F (-37°C)
Evergreen	yes
Bloom time	late spring/early summer
Spread speed	rapid
Sun exposure	part sun to full shade
Soil type	moist, well-draining
Native range	North America

Stonecrop is an easy-to-grow, shade-loving evergreen groundcover. It is native to much of eastern North America. It has blue-green succulent foliage that trails across the ground and forms a dense mat. It can quickly fill in an area where other plants fail to live.

This is a small plant, just a few inches high including the flower stalk. The flowers look like little white stars. It blooms in late spring and the more sun you give it, the more prolifically it flowers.

It can grow in most any light condition from sun to shade, but it prefers to be in part-shade. This versatile little plant can grow in moist conditions, but is also reasonably drought-tolerant. It can thrive under black walnut trees and in the dry shade among thirsty surface tree roots.

Stonecrop is easy to move and transplant. Pull up a piece with roots attached and place it on the soil surface and sprinkle a little extra soil on top. Propagate it by breaking off any section and placing it on bare ground—most of the time it will take hold and take off.

Stonecrop can scramble over gentle slopes and rocks. It can quickly invade gravel path-ways and driveways, so be careful placing it next to such an area, unless you want it to fill in there.

Deer do not care for stonecrop, nor is it bothered by any major pests or diseases. A variety of pollinators visit the flowers.

Interesting Tidbit

Stonecrop is a good choice to place between pavers as it can take a little foot traffic. It also is useful in miniature gardens, rock gardens, and on green roofs.

Noteworthy Cultivars/Varieties

Several other low-growing sedum species also make great groundcovers, although most other sedums do best in full- to part-sun. A few sun-loving sedum groundcovers to try include:

- 'Angelina' stonecrop (*Sedum rupestre* 'Angelina') has tiny yellow flowers and gold-green leaves that turn a bronze shade in cold temperatures.
- Chinese sedum (*Sedum tetractinum* 'Coral Reef') is not as hardy in colder climates as other sedums, but does well in mild/temperate climates. It has yellow-orange coloring and a pleasing round form.
- Blue spruce sedum (*Sedum reflexum*) has blue-green leaves that resemble spruce needles and yellow flowers.

Stachys byzantina

LAMB'S EAR, WOOLLY HEDGENETTLE, WOOLY BETONY

Lamb's Ear *Stachys byzantina*

Height	1-2 feet (30-60 cm)
Winter hardiness	-25°F (-32°C)
Evergreen	somewhat
Bloom time	late spring/early summer
Spread speed	moderate
Sun exposure	full sun to part sun
Soil type	well-draining
Native range	Europe/Asia

The silver-gray basal foliage of **Lamb's Ear** spreads along the ground by rhizomes and in early summer it sends up tall wands of purple flowers. Once the flowers are done, cut them back for a tidier garden look.

Lamb's ear is in the mint family (the square stem is a clue) and that is your indication also that this is a fast spreader when given the chance.

The soft, fuzzy leaves of this plant make it a favorite for children's gardens and sensory learning. That fuzziness also makes it unpalatable to deer and rabbits.

It prefers full sun and a well-draining soil. It can be planted on mild slopes and along sidewalk edges. A bit of foot traffic does not bother it and it bounces back well.

Lamb's ear is pretty shallow-rooted making it easy to dig and divide. Remove sections in spring or fall to fill in other areas or gift it to other gardeners.

It is considered semi-evergreen as the leaves can shrivel up and die back in cold winters. Remove any spent foliage in early spring to prepare the plant for the new growing season.

Lamb's ear does not tolerate wet conditions for long or high humidity. It is happiest when planted where it can get good air circulation around it. Once established, it is fairly drought-tolerant.

It attracts pollinators and is often planted in butterfly gardens. Lamb's ear is also used in xeriscaping and for fire-wise landscapes.

Interesting Tidbit

Lamb's ear is often mistaken for rose campion (*Silene coronaria*) and vice versa. The main difference is the flower. Lamb's ear has a stalk covered in rows of purple or pink blooms, while rose campion has a pink or white flower at the very tip of a tall stalk. The foliage of rose campion (formerly known as *Lychnis coronaria*) is in basal rosettes and lamb's ear is more in upright clumps. Lamb's ear leaves is also much fluffier and a paler silver-gray than rose campion's hairy, gray-green foliage.

Noteworthy Cultivars/Varieties

- 'Silver Carpet' is a top choice for groundcover use as it rarely blooms.
- 'Big Ears' has large leaves. It is also sold under the names 'Countess Helen von Stein' or 'Helene von Stein'.
- Dwarf pink lamb's ear (*Stachys maxima*) has pink flowers and bright green foliage, without the silver fuzz of classic lamb's ear.

DWARF COMFREY, IBERIAN COMFREY, COMPHREY

Dwarf Comfrey *Symphytum ibericum*

Height	1 foot (30 cm)
Winter hardiness	-20°F (-30°C)
Evergreen	no
Bloom time	early summer
Spread speed	moderate
Sun exposure	full sun to part shade
Soil type	moist, well-draining
Native range	Europe

Dwarf Comfrey makes an impenetrable groundcover that is wonderful for swallowing leaves and blocking out weeds. It spreads by underground roots and forms mounds of dark-green leaves. The flowers are clusters of peachy-yellow bells on the end of tall, nodding stocks.

It can grow from full sun to part shade, with reports that it even thrives in full shade. It is not picky about soil types and is drought-tolerant once established. It is in the borage family and has many similarities to that perennial herb.

Comfrey is an efficient soil nutrient accumulator. After the first flush of flowers, chop the plants down and spread the pieces around for an excellent garden mulch. Comfrey "manure" is a rich source of calcium and manganese. Add it to your compost pile as well as the comfrey leaves act as a bio-activator. The plants will regrow quickly.

It can quickly cover an open area and does well on slopes and hillsides for erosion control.

It is easily propagated by root cuttings or division. It is difficult to remove all the roots when transplanting it and it will return, so plant it in a spot where you intend to keep it.

Dwarf comfrey is a pollinator powerhouse plant. Adding it near your vegetable garden encourages bees to pollinate your nearby tomatoes and other plants as well. Beekeepers will especially want to cultivate this groundcover near their hives.

It is a desirable groundcover for use under fruit trees and berry bushes. The comfrey's root systems don't compete with that of the trees and shrubs. A solid groundcover of dwarf comfrey eliminates the need to weed-whack and mow around the fruit-bearing plants, which protects them from possible mechanical injury.

Deer do not find it palatable and it is free of serious disease and pest issues.

Noteworthy Cultivars/Varieties

- 'Hidcote Blue' (which is sometimes known as *Symphytum grandiflorum* 'Hidcote Blue') grows to 18-inches (46 cm) tall and has bright-blue flowers.

Interesting Tidbit

According to plant expert Barbara Melera, "Comfrey's most-significant qualities are related to what the plant does for garden soil. The fat roots aerate heavy clay soils, breaking them up into much more-amenable loam."

Viola spp.

WILD VIOLET, FRAGRANT SWEET VIOLET, COMMON VIOLET, ENGLISH VIOLET, FLORIST'S VIOLET, GARDEN VIOLET

Wild Violet *Viola* spp.

Height	4-6 inches (10-15 cm)
Winter hardiness	-25°F (-32°C)
Evergreen	somewhat
Bloom time	early spring
Spread speed	moderate
Sun exposure	full sun to full shade
Soil type	moist, well-draining
Native range	North America/Europe/Asia

Wild Violet is maligned as a weed (similar to the persecution of clover) by the lawncare industry. It outcompetes turfgrass in many situations, so it is the bane of promoters of a grass monoculture, but if it is a successful groundcover in your landscape, why fight it? It is soft to step on, resilient, an attractive deep-green, and never needs mowing.

Wild violet is a sweet little wildflower with heart-shaped foliage. Its tiny purple, white, or yellow flowers are a pollinator favorite and it is the host plant for several kinds of butterflies. Ground-foraging birds eat the seeds.

It makes a nice groundcover in a woodland garden and is virtually no care—except to cut back the ground-level brown flowers to prevent seeding, if you do not want it to self-sow.

Wild violet also expands in clumps through underground rhizomes. Dig and divide these anytime from spring through fall to spread the plant around your landscape. Plant the rhizome pieces shallowly (a few inches below the soil level).

It can go dormant in extreme drought, heat, and cold, but emerges again when conditions become favorable again.

Wild violet is somewhat deer-resistant and free of any major pests or diseases. The tough, waxy leaves also make them resistant to many herbicides.

Interesting Tidbit

Wild violet flowers and foliage are edible and are a favorite of plant foragers, because they are tasty and high in vitamin C. Make grape-flavored purple syrup from the flowers to enliven a cocktail or to add a fun coloring to baked goods.

Noteworthy Cultivars/Varieties

The pansy and viola are highly bred cultivars of annual violets. There are hundreds of wild violet species. Here are a few hardier varieties:

- 'Wellsiana' (*Viola odorata* 'Wellsiana') is a cultivar of the common violet native to Europe and Asia. It is a compact plant with dark-green leaves and deep-purple flowers. It earned the Royal Horticultural Society's Award of Garden Merit.
- Confederate violet (*Viola sororia* f. *priceana*) is native to North America and has white flowers with purple streaking.
- Canadian white violet (*Viola canadensis*) is native to North America and has white flowers with a yellow center and purple coloring on the backs of the top petals.

6 COVERING GROUND IF NOTHING WILL GROW THERE

Let's face it, there are spaces where next to no plants will thrive. They may be pitch-black or have rock hard ground. Perhaps there was an herbicide spill or remnants of a road salt pile in that spot or some other reason why the soil would kill anything planted there.

When nothing at all can grow in a spot, we get creative. That is when we look at covering bare ground with materials other than living ones. Make a seating area on top of hardscaping there. Put landscape cloth down, edge the area, and pour pea gravel in or set a pattern of bricks or pavers into the surface. Ensure it is fairly level then add your furniture. Place a bistro set or a few chairs with a small table in between to hold your drinks and snacks. Don't forget to add a bit of greenery with a potted plant.

If the area is too narrow for a group seating spot, try a simple bench with or without a back on it. Set a few pavers under the bench and maybe use the space under it for additional storage.

Map out pathways on these too-narrow spaces where plants do not grow well. There is a theory in urban planning called "desire paths" where you watch how people access and cross though an area and note how natural paths get worn in, then you place the sidewalks and walkways in them. In your own landscape, there are likely spots where you walk off designated paths. Place formal paving or stepping stones along them.

Another use of "no grow" areas is as garden storage. Place a shed or outbuilding there. Stack firewood, unused pots (overturned), or designate it as your rock collection pile. A potting bench is another option for a spot where nothing will grow. You can also use this as a place to lean large garden tools like a wheelbarrow, ladder, or a wagon that don't fit inside a shed.

Mulch piles or compost areas are another solution for corners of your landscape where it is difficult to get plants growing. Build or purchase dividers or cages to contain the materials while they break down so they are kept tidy.

◄ Full sun landscapes can be equally as challenging as full shade to cover—even more so where buildings and larger plants create shadows and pockets of shade.

▲ When nothing can grow in a pot, such as under the deep shade of an evergreen tree, consider seating and other solutions.

I use a dead area of my landscape as a "pot ghetto." This is where newly arrived or quarantined plants go until I find a place to put them in the landscape. A tarp or tray underneath them helps to corral them and keeps them from sending roots into the soil if I forget about them for a few months.

Other uses include a children's playhouse, swing sets, or other sports/game equipment areas. Spread a thick layer of bark mulch underneath them to cushion the play space.

Pets also deserve a designated outdoor area to explore and be safe in. Site a dog run, rabbit hutch, or catio (screened outdoor cat room) in an out of the way spot that is not hospitable for plantings.

Finally, think art. Set up an area to display sculptures or a collection of decorative objects. Groupings of almost any item can be gathered into a bare spot and highlighted with outdoor lighting. Position them on risers or columns to give them an elevated profile and deliberate display.

▶ Groundcovers are charming planted in cracks and openings in patios, terraces, and verandas. They also prevent weeds from creeping into these spots.

▼ **Overleaf:** Mondo grass is an ideal groundcover that can take light foot traffic and stays good-looking virtually year-round.

SOURCES AND RESOURCES

Here are a few resources and sources for groundcovers. Purchasing the plants suggested in this book may not always be possible as not all of the plants will be available in all countries and some will be banned from import due to their aggressive nature. However, there is likely a similar species or equivalent that you can source in your area.

Join a garden club or plant society in your area. (Or start one if there isn't one!) Most garden-related groups host plant swaps among their members or encourage direct plant trades. If a plant is successful in other local gardens, it should also be in yours. Further, if a plant is robust enough for a gardener to dig and divide it—that is a good indication that it may be a good groundcover candidate. Be alert for any plants that are described at these swaps as aggressive-spreaders.

For these same reasons, attend local plant sales hosted by garden clubs and plant societies. Many of the plants at these sales were dug from members' gardens.

Ask around. Your neighbors, coworkers, family, and friends may have groundcovers that they are willing to share with you. Fellow gardeners are generous by nature and if you ask nicely they are almost always willing to share their hellebore seedlings or straying rhizomes of creeping Jenny. Online forums for neighborhood and civic groups are also a fine spot to ask for extra plant divisions.

Visit local public gardens at home and also on your travels. Public gardens are a terrific resource for garden ideas and research. They offer inspiration and examples that you can take photos of and use in your own home landscape.

▲ Plant swaps and similar events are terrific sources of groundcovers for free or next to it.

Take pictures of plant labels and close-ups of the plantings as well so you can research them when you get home.

Shop at local, independent garden centers. The owners and employees of these businesses know their inventories well and can advise you on groundcover choices for your region. Some even have installation services that will come and put in the plants for you. Visit them at a non-busy time (for example not on the Saturday of the Mother's Day weekend) to discuss the various options they may be able to offer.

There are many excellent online and mail-order garden retail and wholesale sellers as well. On page 172, you'll find a list of a few to get you started. This list is by no means comprehensive, these are the ones I have purchased or received samples from personally and can attest to their quality.

▲ A sample display of various groundcovers shows the many textures and colors available in retail nurseries.

Recommended Groundcover Nurseries

American Meadows www.americanmeadows.com

Bluestone Perennials www.bluestoneperennials.com

Classic Groundcovers www.classic-groundcovers.com

Classy Groundcovers https://classygroundcovers.com

Great Garden Plants www.greatgardenplants.com

Jeepers Creepers www.jeeperscreepers.info (does not sell directly, but has a store locator)

Mountain Moss www.mountainmoss.com

North Creek Nurseries www.northcreeknurseries.com

Stepables www.stepables.com (does not sell directly, but has a store locator)

Sunshine Farm & Gardens https://sunfarm.com

Treadwell Plants www.treadwellplants.com

In addition to the above list, **All About Groundcover Inc.,** located in Grove City, PA, is a wholesale grower/rewholesaler. They do not have a website, but can be reached by phone at 814-786-7024.

Finally, I find this **online groundcover plant spacing calculator** to be helpful when estimating how many plants to order: https://classygroundcovers.com/site/page?view=plantCalculator.

ABOUT THE AUTHOR

Kathy Jentz is editor and publisher of the award-winning *Washington Gardener Magazine*, based in Washington, DC. She is also the editor of three plant society journals: *Water Garden Journal* (IWGS), *The Azalean* (ASA), and *Fanfare* (Daylily Society Region 3).

Currently, she is the President of the Silver Spring Garden Club and is on the board of several other garden clubs and organizations.

She hosts of the popular GardenDC Podcast, which was recently named Best DC Podcast.

She is coauthor of *The Urban Garden: 101 Ways to Grow Food and Beauty in the City* (also published by Cool Springs Press).

Her mission is to turn black thumbs green. A life-long gardener, Kathy believes that growing plants should be stress-free and enjoyable. Her philosophy is inspiration over perspiration.

Photo by Zoe Zindasha

Where to find Kathy Jentz:
Twitter www.twitter.com/WDCGardener
Instagram www.instagram.com/wdcgardener/
Pinterest www.pinterest.com/wdcgardener/boards/
Podcast: *GardenDC* https://anchor.fm/gardendc/
Blog www.washingtongardener.blogspot.com
Facebook www.facebook.com/WashingtonGardenerMagazine/
YouTube www.youtube.com/washingtongardenermagazine
Online Store www.amazon.com/shop/wdcgardener

ACKNOWLEDGMENTS

This book was born from a talk suggested by a garden club member, who asked me to share my favorite groundcovers with her group. I had been trialing various groundcovers in my turf-free landscape for several years and the talk outline flowed effortlessly. It quickly became one of my most popular speaking topics and I have incorporated all of the wonderful audience feedback and suggestions into this book.

My sincere gratitude goes to my family and friends for all of your support in my garden writing career. My garden mentors and teachers have been many and they are too numerous to name here, but I want to single out a few special influences.

Thank you to my paternal grandmother who shared her hollyhock seeds and love of African violets. Thank you to my maternal grandmother who let me rearrange her garden gnomes and pluck whatever herbs I wished to gather into little fragrant bouquets. Thank you to my fellow gardeners who gifted me plant divisions and seeds over the years filling my garden with memories, bounty, and blooms.

Finally, thank you to my parents who had me weeding and watering in their garden from an early age—even though I protested the hard work at the time, I am blessed and happy to have been able to learn and grow under their care.

PHOTO CREDITS

All photography by **Kathy Jentz**, except:

Janet Davis on pp. 35, 158–159;

Susan Harris on pp. 52–53;

Iseli Nurseries on p. 120;

JLY Gardens on pp. 16, 19, 31, 143, 174;

R. Theo Margelony on pp. 63 (bottom);

Christina Salwitz on pp. 11, 34, 36 (right), 37 (top), 136–137;

Shutterstock on pp. 14–15, 20, 26–27, 37 (bottom), 59, 69–71, 74, 75, 77 (bottom), 80, 83, 94–95, 97, 100–101, 122–123, 127, 128, 135, 162–163, 167–169, 176;

and

George Weigel on pp. 36 (left), 72, 164

INDEX

THE **URBAN GARDEN**

101 Ways to Grow Food
and Beauty in the City

KATHY JENTZ + TERI SPEIGHT

THE URBAN GARDEN

978-0760373019